Thomas Willis
1621-1675

His Life and Work

J. T. Hughes

Rimes House
Oxford
2009

Thomas Willis 1621 – 1675
His Life and Work
J. T. Hughes

Second edition in 2009 by
Rimes House
2 Bishop Kirk Place
Oxford OX2 7HJ

First published in 1991 by
Royal Society of Medicine Services Limited
1 Wimpole Street London W1M 8AE
8 East 60th Street New York NY 10022

British Library Cataloguing in Publication Data
A catalogue record for this book is available from the British Library.

     Thomas Willis 1621-1675: his life and work.
     Hughes, J.T. 1928-

1. Thomas Willis. 2. Biography. 3. Medical History. 4. 17th Century Science.

ISBN 978-1-874317-03-6

Typeset in Sabon and printed in Great Britain by
The Holywell Press Ltd
15-17 Kings Meadow
Ferry Hinksey Road
Oxford OX2 ODP

To my wife, Catherine

LIST OF ILLUSTRATIONS

CHRONOLOGY OF WILLIS'S LIFE, WORK, AND TIMES

1621   Born 27 January at Great Bedwyn, Wiltshire.

1625   James I died and succeeded by Charles I.

1631   Death of Rachel, Willis's mother.

1636   Plague prevalent, causing Court to move to Woodstock. Willis matriculated at Christ Church, Oxford, aged 16.

1639   18 June. Willis graduated BA, Oxford, aged 18.

1642   18 June. Willis proceeded MA, Oxford, aged 21.

1643   4 August. Father and stepmother died of camp fever during the siege of Oxford.

1644   Moved to North Hinksey due to disturbances in Oxford.

1645   Back in Oxford. Enlisted in Dover's regiment in the service of the King.

1646   24 June. Sir Thomas Glenham surrendered Oxford, to Fairfax.

        8 December. Graduated BM, Oxford. Began medical practice.

1649   30 January. Execution of Charles I.

        14 December. Revival of Ann Green by Willis and William Petty.

1657   7 April. Married Mary Fell in St Michael's Church, Oxford, aged 36.

1658   3 September. Death of Oliver Cromwell.

1659   Publication of first book, *Diatribae duae medico-philosophicae*.

1660   Restoration of Charles II.

        25 August. Elected Sedleian Professor of Natural Philosophy, University of Oxford.

        30 October. Doctor of Medicine, by request of Charles II.

1663   Elected Fellow of Royal Society.

1664   Published *Cerebri Anatome*. Elected Fellow of Royal College of Physicians.

1667   Published *Pathologiae Cerebri*. Moved to London.

1670   31 October. His wife Mary died, and was buried in Westminster Abbey.

        Published *Affectionum quae dicuntur hystericae et hypochondriacae*.

1672   1 September. Married Elizabeth Calley in Westminster Abbey.

        Published *De Anima Brutorum*.

1674   Published part 1 of *Pharmaceuticae Rationalis*.

1675   11 November. Died at home in St Martin's Lane, and was buried in Westminster Abbey.

        Part 2 of *Pharmaceuticae Rationalis* published.

1691   Posthumous publication of tract on plague written in 1666.

ACKNOWLEDGEMENTS

I AM INDEBTED for help in this work to many people and institutions. Any biographer stands on the shoulders of his predecessors and I must mention my indebtedness to several. The late Kenneth Dewhurst wrote many papers on Willis, two books reproducing in translation Willis's lectures and casebook, and valuable biographies of John Locke and Thomas Sydenham. Dewhurst loved to talk about Willis, his favourite physician, and I profited by his friendship. The late Alfred Meyer, a neuropathological colleague of an earlier generation to mine, and who guided my first steps into our common subject, spent part of his retirement in researching the neuro-anatomical works of Willis, ably assisted by Raymond Hierons, who continues this enquiry. I have read with pleasure and instruction the works of Hansruedi Isler. Robert G Frank Jr is the author of the notice in the *Dictionary of Scientific Biography* and has also included much on Willis in his book *Harvey and the Oxford Physiologists*. To William Feindel, I am grateful for his papers on Willis and also for the research published in his facsimile edition of Pordage's translation of *Cerebri Anatome*.

Having worked in the Oxford Hospitals and in the University of Oxford for the past 35 years, I am deeply in their debt for library facilities. The Cairns Library in the Radcliffe Infirmary and its librarian, Mr Robin Snowball, have ever been helpful, notably in the use, through Mr Snowball, of the British Lending Library. I have made great use of the Bodleian Library, the Ashmolean Museum, and the libraries of St Johns, Merton, and Christ Church, in the last of which Mr Wing has been helpful in many ways. Further afield, I have been welcome in London at the libraries of the Royal Society and the Royal College of Physicians, and at the British Library, and the Wellcome Library. In Washington DC, I have used the Library of Congress, and the Folger Shakespeare Library, where I was permitted to examine John Ward's diary.

The Keeper of the Oxford University Archives has allowed me to peruse and reproduce many of the entries relating to Willis, and I have similarly used the Record Offices of Wiltshire, Oxfordshire, and Berkshire. The Public Record Office in London has allowed me to see the will of Willis, part of which is reproduced here. The Dean and Chapter of Westminster have provided a photograph of Willis's gravestone in the Abbey.

For photographic work I am chiefly indebted to the studios of the Bodleian Library and the Ashmolean Museum. Mr Dudley, of the Ashmolean Musuem, has produced the majority of the illustrations used here, the excellence of which is evident.

Finally, I wish to thank for many discussions my old chief, Dr AHT Robb-Smith, Dr WC Gibson of Vancouver, and the group of Oxford medical historians at the Wellcome Unit at Oxford, formerly led by Dr C Webster, whose book *The Great Instauration* has been an inspiration, as well as providing a mine of information.

CONTEMPORARY SOURCES AND BIOGRAPHERS

THE MAJOR BODY of information on the life of Thomas Willis is based on a few primary sources, namely the writings of John Fell, John Aubrey, Anthony Wood, and Browne Willis. These sources are detailed below, to which are added references to the principal modern biographies of Willis. Other information on the life of Willis is obtained from the text of his works and there are incidental observations from his many friends and colleagues.

John Fell (1625-1686)[1] was a contemporary of Willis in the University at Oxford, and served alongside Willis in the Royalist forces. He was a lifelong friend, and became a relation when Willis married his sister, Mary. As the manuscript of Willis's *Pharmaceutice Rationalis* was being printed, news came from London of the death of Willis. Fell, then Bishop of Oxford, added a three page postscript in Latin to the printed work which forms a valuable obituary.

John Aubrey (1626-1697),[2] an antiquary, and collector of books, biographical details, and folklore, was educated at Trinity College, Oxford, and was the junior of Willis in Oxford by a few years. Aubrey amassed many papers but, during his lifetime, only his *Miscellanies* was published, in 1696. His papers were edited by Anthony Wood and 'Letters to Eminent Persons' subsequently appeared in an edition in 1813. Aubrey's papers were further edited in an 1898 edition, in which the relevant information on Willis appears in volume 2.

Anthony Wood (1632-1695),[3,4] who later styled himself Anthony A Wood, lived his whole life in Oxford. Having a private income, he devoted his adult life to historical and biographical studies, gathering a large body of data, much of which was eventually published. He was born in a house opposite the gate of Merton College, in which he lived throughout his life, and where he died. For several years, Willis was a neighbour of Wood in the adjacent house of Beam Hall. Wood was educated at New College school in Oxford, Thame School in Oxfordshire, and Merton College of the University of Oxford. He seems to have been a difficult man, who made enemies easily, and never gained a College Fellowship in Oxford. He began work on a history of the County of Oxfordshire but this was never completed, and he turned to the writing of a history of the University of Oxford. This work was published in 1674, as *Historic et Antiquitates Universitatis Oxoniensis*, having been translated into Latin by the delegates of the University Press. Wood disliked the Latin translation, and rewrote the work in English with many additions, the vernacular version being published after his death by John Gutch in 1792-1796 under the title *The History and Antiquities of the University of Oxford*. Wood himself published *Athenae Oxonienses; an Exact history of all the Writers and Bishops who, had their Education in Oxford from 1500 to 1690, to which are added the Fasti or Annals for the said time*, a most valuable collection of biographies of Oxford notables, and of events between 1500 and 1690, the substance of which appeared in several later editions. Wood did not content himself with the bare facts of the lives of his subjects but included critical judgements, some of which were considered libellous, and resulted in his expulsion from the University of Oxford. His account of Willis is most valuable as he was Willis's neighbour and knew him well, but as he seems to have disliked Willis, allowance must be made for this animosity.

Browne Willis (1682-1760),[5] Thomas Willis's grandson, attended Westminster School, proceeded to Christ Church, Oxford, and then studied law at the Inner Temple, London. He was member of Parliament for the borough of Buckingham from 1705-1708, after which, he devoted most of his time to the study of antiquities, and to the history of the cathedrals of England and Wales in particular. He was proud of his famous grandfather, and created or renewed several memorials to him, but his most important biographical document concerning Willis was a letter he sent in 1725 to Bishop Kennet, which was afterwards discovered in Bishop Kennet's copy of Anthony Wood's *Athenae* and incorporated in later editions, as in the edition by Philip Bliss in 1817.

Willis has attracted several short biographies in addition to which many articles, dealing with his contribution to a specific medical subject, have included biographical notes. In the late eighteenth century an account of Willis appeared in *Biographica Britannica*,[6] and the Willis family was described in *Collectanea Topographica Genealogica* in 1843.[7] Willis appeared in the 1878 *Munk's Roll of the Fellows of the Royal College of Physicians*[8] and in the 1917 *Dictionary of National Biography*.[9] Modern biographies by Feindel in 1965,[10] by Frank in 1976,[11] and by Dewhurst in 1980,[12] have been published but the only substantial biography, written originally in German, is by Dr Hansruedi Isler. This was published in 1965, followed by an English translation by the author in 1968.[13]

REFERENCES

1   John Fell. *Postscript to Pharmaceutice Rationalis*, Part 2. London, 1684. (The postscript, written in 1675, consists of three unnumbered pages after the preface to the reader.)

2   John Aubrey. *Brief Lives Chiefly of Contemporaries, Set Down by John Aubrey, Between the Years 1669-1696*, Vol 2, edited by Andrew Clark. Oxford: 1898, pp 302-4.

3   Anthony Wood (1632-1695). *The Life and Times of Anthony Wood*, Vol 2, edited by Andrew Clark. Oxford: 1892, p 326.

4   Anthony Wood (1632-1695). *Athenae Oxoniensis . . .*, 2nd edn Vol 2. edited by Philip Bliss. London: 1721, pp 549-51.

5   Browne Willis: The best biographical source is Browne Willis's letter to Bishop Kennet dated 7 March 1725 and reproduced in the 1817 edition of Anthony Wood's *Athenae Oxoniensis*, Vol 3, edited by Philip Bliss. London: 1813-1820, pp 1048-53.

6   *Biographica Britannica*, Vol 6, Part 2. London: 1776, pp 4291-7.

7   *Collectanea Topographica Genealogica*, Vol 5. London: 1843, p 31.

8 W Munk. *The Roll of the Royal College of Physicians of London*, 2nd edn, Vol 1. London: 1878, pp 338-42.

9 *Dictionary of National Biography*, Vol 21. London: 1917, pp 496-7.

10 W Feindel. *Thomas Willis: The Anatomy of the Brain and Nerves*. Montreal: McGill University Press, 1964. (This Tercentenary Edition 1664-1964 includes a biography of Willis in Vol 1 on pp 7-14.)

11 RG Frank, Jr. Willis, Thomas. In: *Dictionary of Scientific Biography*, Vol XIV, edited by CG Gillispie. New York: Charles Scribner's Sons, 1976.

12 K Dewhurst. *Thomas Willis's Oxford Lectures*. Oxford: Sandford Publications, 1980. (This translation of Willis's lectures is preceded by a biography on pp 1-36.)

13 H Isler. *Thomas Willis 1621-1675: Doctor and Scientist*. London, New York: Hafner, 1968.

CONTENTS

Index

Chapter 1

Introduction

The history of the world is but the biography of great men
Thomas Carlyle, 1789-1881

The life of Thomas Willis (1621-1675) coincided with remarkable political, religious, and cultural changes, which were as conspicuous in England as in any other country. Scientific discoveries were also evident in this century and also notably in England. Willis was a typical product of mid-seventeenth century England, and it is interesting, to briefly consider some relevant events in this and in the preceding century.

The immediate impression of the sixteenth century[1,2] is that of discovery, seen in many areas of enquiry, and due, seemingly, to the development in many European countries of an overwhelming curiosity. The explosive growth of geographical discovery by sea began just at the end of the fifteenth century with voyages to the Bahamas, Cuba, and Haiti by Columbus in 1492, to Nova Scotia by Cabot in 1497, to Calicut by da Gama in 1498, and to Venezuela by Vespucci in 1499. The development by Gutenberg of printing using movable type faces, from about 1445, had a conspicuous effect on the dissemination of knowledge, which by the mid-sixteenth century had produced some innovative scientific texts. In 1540 the *De la Pirotechnica* of Vannoccio Biringuccio appeared dealing with the technology of industrial processes such as metal smelting, and distillation, whilst in the year 1543 the magnificent *De Humani Corporis Fabrica* of Andreas Vesalius described and illustrated modern anatomy, based on human dissections. In the same year the heliocentric nature of the solar system was communicated to scholars in the *De Revolutionibus Orbium Coelestium* by Nicolaus Copernicus. Thus three books of the greatest importance to science appeared within three years, and near the mid-point of the sixteenth century.

The scientific curiosity of the sixteenth and seventeenth centuries was evident in England and manifested in Oxford in a large expansion of academic scholarship including the beginnings of scientific research.[3,4] The number of students at Oxford had been slowly rising towards the end of the sixteenth century and this rise was continued at the beginning of the seventeenth.

Oxford accommodated these new students by the expansion of existing colleges and the creation of new colleges. The sixteenth century saw the foundation of Brasenose in 1509, Corpus Christi in 1517, Christ Church in 1546, Trinity in 1554-1555, St John's in 1555, and Jesus in 1571. This creation of new colleges was continued in the early seventeenth century with the foundation of Wadham in 1613, and Pembroke in 1624. By this time, Oxford University was admitting

1

more than 400 students annually, and as many as 240 were graduating BA, and 150 MA, in 1660.

Medical discoveries mainly awaited the seventeenth century and 1628 saw the publication of the *Exercitatio Anatomica de Motu Cordis et Sanguinis* by William Harvey, possibly the most important single publication in medicine. Thus Willis, born in 1625, and entering the practice of medicine at the mid-point of the seventeenth century, began his own scientific work on a modern basis of many revolutionary discoveries in medical science, the most notable being the discovery of the circulation of the blood by Harvey.

The politics of seventeenth century England[5,6] was characterised by a widespread revolt against authority, and during the lifetime of Willis, there were striking changes. A few weeks before the birth of Willis, in January 1621, James I in making his opening speech to Parliament, requested substantial funds for his foreign policy, but declined to give explanations, maintaining that the conduct of foreign policy was a matter for the royal prerogative. Parliament retaliated with a wholly inadequate financial grant, and turned the debate to their more favoured subject of domestic grievances. When James died in 1625, the struggle between King and Parliament was well advanced, and soon embroiled his son, Charles I, in a contest of power, which led to the Petition of Right in 1628, the dismissal of Parliament by Charles, in 1629,11 years of rule

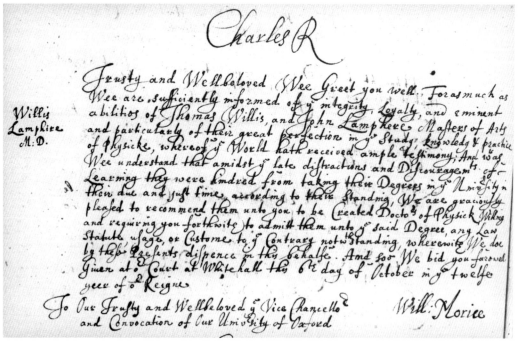

Copy of a letter from Charles II, requesting the University of Oxford to grant Willis the degree of Doctor of Medicine (University of Oxford, OU Archives, NEP/supra/Reg.Ta, f. 26).

without parliament, and then in 1640, the summoning of the belligerent Long Parliament. This was the last parliament of Charles I and it was his attempt to arrest the Five Members which was the prelude to the Civil War (1642-1645), ending with the defeat of the forces of the King at Naseby in June 1645 and the execution of Charles I on 30 January 1649.

Oxford, for the greater part of the Civil War,[7] was the headquarters of the King, and Willis was personally concerned in the struggle, being enrolled in an auxiliary regiment raised by the Earl of Dover to defend the City.[8]

The period of the Commonwealth and Protectorate, from 1649-1660, was a difficult one for Willis, since he was a Royalist and wished to preserve the old rites of the Book of Common Prayer, now forbidden under the rule of the Puritans, who had introduced the Presbyterian Directory. He was later to marry Mary Fell, the daughter of the Dean of Christ Church, who with her family was ejected from the Deanery, following the imprisonment of the Dean. The Dean, Samuel Fell, was at that time the Vice Chancellor of the University, and wished to uphold the forbidden church services. It is probable that the difficulty of pursuing the form of religion hitherto customary in Oxford turned Willis from a career in divinity to one in medicine. John Fell, the son of Samuel Fell, put the choice of Willis in these words:

> . . . the cause of the Best Prince being overcome, Cromwell's Tyranny afforded to this wretched Nation a Peace more cruel than any War. From thence, the Church being trampled on, and Divinity together with the Divines suppressed, he applied himself to the study of Physick, in which, in a short time he made eminent progress.

The restoration of Charles II in 1660 swiftly reversed Willis's fortunes and on 8 August 1660 he was appointed to the Sedleian chair of Natural Philosophy, and given the degree of doctor of medicine on 30 October that year.

This historical summary shows how political events during the early life of Willis, directed his energies to medicine, and how he experienced two changes in fortune. The first was a reversal during the Commonwealth and Protectorate, from 1649-1660, whilst the second was a benefit in that, with the restoration of the monarchy in 1660, Charles II conferred certain academic distinctions on Willis, as a reward for loyalty to his father, Charles I.

REFERENCES

1   JD Mackie. The earlier Tudors, 1485-1558. In: *The Oxford History of England*, Vol VII, edited by Sir George Clark. Oxford: Clarendon Press, 1952.
2   JB Black. The reign of Elizabeth, 1558-1603. In: *The Oxford History of England*, 2nd edn Vol VIII, edited by Sir George Clark, Oxford: Clarendon Press, 1959.

3   P Allen. Medical education in 17th century England, *Journal of the History of Medicine and Allied Sciences*, 1946, Vol 1, pp 115-43.

4   P Allen. Scientific studies in the English Universities of the Seventeenth century, *Journal of History and Ideas*, 1949, Vol 10, pp 219-53.

5   G Davies. The early Stuarts, 1603-1660. In: *The Oxford History of England*, 2nd edn, Vol IX, edited by Sir George Clark. Oxford: Clarendon Press, 1959.

6   G Clark. The later Stuarts, 1660-1714. In : *The Oxford History of England*, 2nd edn, Vol. X, edited by Sir George Clark. Oxford: Clarendon Press, 1956.

7   FJ Varley. *The Siege of Oxford*. Oxford, 1932.

8   M Toynbee and P Young. *Strangers in Oxford*. London: Chichester, 1973.

Chapter 2

Birth, Childhood, and Early Education

Extracted from an honest family
John Fell, 1675

Thomas Willis was to live most of his life in Oxford, except for the last nine years which were spent in London, but he was born, in January 1621, at Great Bedwyn in Wiltshire. The ancestors of a man, who advanced medicine so profoundly, naturally arouse curiosity. A few details are uncertain and so for this account, I have examined the contemporary documents cited earlier (pp xii and xiii) and consulted the baptismal, marriage, and burial records in the library of Merton College, the Bodleian Library, and in the Oxfordshire, Berkshire, and Wiltshire Record Offices.

There is good evidence that several generations of the Willis family came from Church Hanborough and Long Hanborough, adjacent villages in Oxfordshire a few miles north-west of Oxford, and this was also the opinion of Browne Willis, the grandson of Thomas Willis. It is significant that the land in these villages belonged to St John's College, Oxford, and probably the Willis families farmed as tenants of the college. St John's College was founded in 1555 by Sir Thomas White, Kt, Alderman of the City of London, and amongst its earliest scholars was Francis Willis (sometimes spelt Wyllys) who was to become a fellow of the college and, in 1577, its president, combining this office with the living of Kingston Bagpuize from 1581, and the deanship of Worcester from 1587. I have found no evidence to connect Willis with Francis Willis but this descent is possible, and Browne Willis considered Francis Willis to be a distant relation who enabled his great grandfather to attend St John's College.

The father of Willis, also called Thomas Willis, son of another Thomas Willis, was probably born in Kennington, a village in Berkshire, near to Oxford. The village of Kennington, Berkshire is near the villages of North and South Hinksey, and Mary the sister of Thomas Willis (father) went to live at South Hinksey as the wife of Thomas Pierce (or Pearce). Thomas Willis (father) courted a girl from North Hinksey named Rachel Howell and they were married around 1600. Rachel Howell was distantly related to William of Wykeham, Bishop of Winchester and the founder of New College, Oxford. Before or after this marriage Thomas Willis (father) was, according to Anthony Wood, the butler to Sir George Stonehouse of Radley. According to John Fell, Thomas Willis (father) became a retainer at St John's College, graduated MA (this is uncertain as the record of this MA has not been found), and qualified as an attorney.

The couple moved to Great Bedwyn in Wiltshire, as Thomas Willis (father) was appointed steward to a landed proprietor, Sir Walter Smith, a position which again confirms a connection with St John's College, which owned land at Great Bedwyn. Thus it was that Willis came to be born in Great Bedwyn, Wiltshire, now a pretty, unspoiled village between Marlborough and Hungerford and some two miles south of the main A4 road to Bath.

Great Bedwyn is a very old settlement in an upland valley with a stream, called the Dun, cutting its way through white chalk hills to join the river Kennet. The name comes from the ancient Celtic in which *bedd* means grave, and *wynn* means white. The 'Place of the White Barrow' is a possible translation, which agrees with the name 'Leucomagus' of the Romans. In the Anglo Saxon chronicle it is given the name of 'Bedanheaford', which may be translated as 'The Grave's Head', whilst it appears in Domesday Book as 'Bedewinde'. In Saxon times it was a place of some importance being the residence of Cissa, the Viceroy of Wiltshire, and, being a borough, sent two members to parliament from the reign of Edward I until the reform of the franchise. At the time of Willis, Great Bedwyn was a prosperous town, based on the wool trade, and had a population of from 1500-2000.

Willis was born on 27 January (old calendar) in the calendar year of 1621 and in the ecclesiastical year of 1620, since the 1621 church year began in April. The year is sometimes given as 1620/1621 but there is no uncertainty concerning the date of birth. The birth place, which still exists, is in Farm Lane, at the north-east end of the village.[1] The house was old at the time of Willis's birth and was an alteration of an older building, probably a small monastic building, surviving from the fifteenth century. There is external evidence of this in a massive chimney stack, now with two chimneys, one of stone and a later addition built in brick, and evidence in the line of plastering of the chimney stack, that the roof was originally much higher. The present roof is thatched. Inside there are massive oak beams, and two huge fireplaces all features relating to an earlier larger building. The building now has two floors with three lower rooms and two rooms above, in one of which, a large bedroom, Willis was probably born. The house is called Ivy Cottage, a name which appears on old maps, but at one time the name was changed to 'The Castle' and the house was used as a guest house.

Willis was baptised on 14 February in the parish Church of St Mary the Virgin, in Great Bedwyn, a Norman building, based on a Saxon church, but now much altered, with much additional building in the nineteenth century. The relevant Parish Register is now in the Wiltshire County Record Office at Trowbridge, but the page containing the baptismal entry for Willis is much defaced.[2] The first culprit was Browne Willis who erased the next entry to insert the following comment:

Willis's birthplace from a print in the Gentlemen's Magazine, 1798. *The double chimney is evidence of an earlier building, probably monastic.*

Willis's birthplace today.

N.b. He was the most Famous Physitian in the World in his tyme & dying Nov. the 11th 1675 in the 54th year of his age, was buried in Westminster Abbey.

Today most of the writing in this page of the register is illegible because someone has applied a solution of gallic acid to the page, to render the faded writing more clear, and with time the whole page has darkened, causing the entry of Willis's baptism to be illegible. However, from other copies we know it to have read: *Thomas Wyllis the sonne of Thomas Willis and Rachell his wyffe was baptysed the xiiij day of February anno predicto.*

North Hinksey Church and Cross. In the chancel of the parish church of St Lawrence, North Hinksey, a stone marks the burial place of Willis's father. Print from the Gentlemen's Magazine, 1817.

Willis lived in Ivy Cottage at Great Bedwyn for eight or nine years by which time his mother, Rachel, inherited an estate of some 50-75 acres at North Hinksey, a small village two miles from the centre of Oxford, but in Berkshire, being on the other side of the river Thames. Thus the family returned to Rachel's home but their fortune in this inheritance was soon tragically interrupted by the death of Rachel in 1631. On 5 July 1631, Rachel was buried in the Parish Church of St Lawrence in North Hinksey. Coincidently, a friend of Thomas Willis (father), named Thomas Ruffin, and who farmed nearby at South Hinksey, died leaving a widow with three sons and two daughters. This double bereavement brought the two families together, and, within a short time, Thomas Willis (father) married the widow Elizabeth Ruffin.

The house in North Hinksey, in which the family lived, still exists in the village, near the church, and is called Ferry Cottage, recalling the North Hinksey ferry, once an important crossing of the river Thames.[3] The house, when I visited, was owned and occupied by the Master of St Cross College, of the University of Oxford. It is a small Elizabethan house, opposite Manor farm, at the point where formerly the road proceeded to North Hinksey ferry. The house is constructed in stone with two bays, with a huge central chimney-stack serving two fireplaces downstairs, back to back. The house has one and one half storeys, since the walls of the upstairs rooms are only 4ft at the eaves. The window openings have ovolu mouldings to the mullions, and rebates in the stonework, where wooden shutters were hung on the outside. The windows were originally unglazed, and some of the iron bars in the windows survive. The entrance to the house is in the south-east wall, and gave access directly into the dining area of the house, with a large open fireplace, and a brick oven for baking bread. Between this room and the back of the house was a dairy or buttery area, and under this and the hall was a large cellar. A short passage leads to the sitting room and a master bedroom. This bedroom has a large open fireplace with a stone mantel with a four-centred arch. By the side of this fireplace, a semi-circular staircase leads to the upper floor, where there are two rooms, partly under the eaves. Behind

A recent photograph of Ferry Cottage, North Hinksey (N Pollard).

the house is a stone-lined well and there are stone remains of former extensive outbuildings. The mouldings and stops on the main beam of the sitting room suggest a date for the house of between 1580 and 1600.

At the time of his mother's death, Willis had commenced school in Oxford, walking from his home in North Hinksey, down Hinksey Lane, and over Botley causeway, constructed in 1540, over the water meadows of Botley, arriving near the centre of Oxford in the street known as 'The High'. From Carfax, the centre of Oxford, along the High, the original building of the school may be identified, on the right-hand side as number 135, and is now a tobacconist. The school was called Sylvester's Academy, the headmaster being Edward Sylvester, a Balliol graduate, with a reputation for classics. Here Willis gained a proficiency in Latin that served him well throughout his life, and also prepared him for matriculation into the University of Oxford.

The details of Willis's tuition in the University of Oxford are taken from the archives of the University. On 3 March 1638, at the age of 16, Willis matriculated into the University of Oxford and entered one of its colleges called Christ Church. The name is confusing since the institution is a college rather than a church. The chapel of the college, formerly the church of Saint Frideswide, was made the cathedral of Oxford in 1542. The corporate designation of the college founded in 1556 is 'The Dean and Chapter of the Cathedral Church of Christ in Oxford of the Foundation of King Henry the Eighth'.

Willis entered Christ Church as a 'batler' which in seventeenth century Oxford was classed in the third group of *pauperes scholares, mediastini*, and were further described as sizars, servitors, batlers (or battelers). The two first groups of higher status were the gentlemen commoners and commoners, who paid for their board and lodging, whilst a servitor or batler would be probably supported by the college or one of the Canons. Willis was servitor to Dr Iles, a Canon of the College, and assisted Mrs Iles. The meagre information of Willis's early days at Christ Church comes from John Aubrey who wrote:

> He was first servitor to Dr (Thomas) Iles, one of the canons of C.C. whose wife was a knowing woman in physic and surgery, and did many cures. Tom Willis then wore a blew livery-cloak, and studied at the lower end of the hall, by the hall-dore; was pretty handy, and his mistress would oftentimes have him to assist her in making of medicines'

Dr Iles and his wife not only assisted Willis in his entry to the University and his support at Christ Church, but influenced his subsequent career. This must also have been the opinion of Browne Willis who erected the memorial tablet in Christ Church Cathedral which reads 'Dr. THOMAS ILES below which appears 'Dr. THOMAS WILLIS'.

M S
THOMAE ILES S.T.P
Hujus Ædis Canonici;
Qui obijt 20 Iunii 1649:
Cujus inter Encomia
non hoc erat minimum,
Quod fub ejus Aufpiciis ac Patrocinio
Academicæ Eruditionis Elementa
Hâc in Æde hauferat
THOMAS WILLIS M D
Literato in Orbe
Notiffimus.
Uiro
De ipfius Avo, etiamque de Patriâ
Optime merito
Hoc parentavit MNEMOSYNON
BW : L L.D.

Memorial Tablet to Canon Thomas Iles and Thomas Willis in Christ Church Cathedral.
Thomas Willis was a Batler at Christ Church and servitor to Canon Iles. Photograph,
taken by Mr Dudley (courtesy of the Dean of Christ Church).

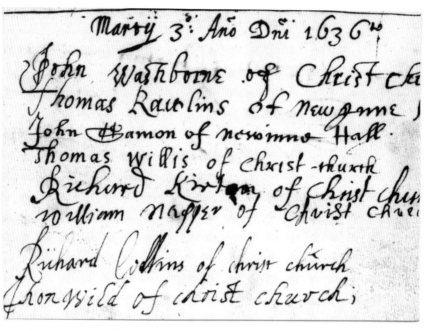

Record of Willis's matriculation in the University of Oxford at Christ Church on 3 March 1636/1637. This is Willis's own signature at the age of 16 (University of Oxford, OU Archives, SP/39).

Although in 1638, when Willis matriculated into the University of Oxford, there were in England (and in Scotland) the stirrings of profound religious and political upheaval, the studies of Willis towards his BA degree followed a course that had not significantly changed for centuries.[4,5] Indeed two years before, in 1636, the Laudian Statutes, had under the direction of Archbishop Laud, confirmed the nature of these studies. Students in the faculty of Arts were obliged to spend four years 'in the study of the Arts and in diligent attendance,

Record of Willis's Bachelor of Arts degree, conferred on 19 June 1639 (University of Oxford, OU Archives, NEP/supra/Reg. Q, f. 214v).

according to the exigence of the statutes, upon the public lectures within the University.' The professors were required to give the lectures personally, each lecture having a duration of at least three quarters of an hour, and delivered slowly and clearly, since the students were obliged to take down the lecture in writing. At the conclusion of the lecture the professor had to 'wait for a time in the schools, and if any scholar or hearer wished to argue against what they had said at lecture, or entertained any doubts on any point they had to listen 'with kindness, and answer the difficulties and doubts proposed to them'. As homework the student had to 'in private diligently to peruse the author whom the public professor in each faculty [had] undertaken to explain'.

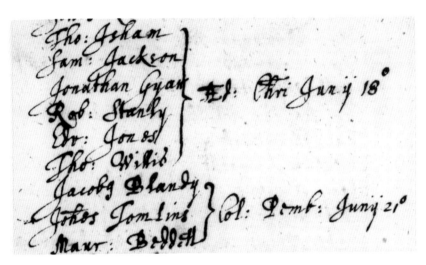

Record of Willis's Master of Arts degree, conferred on 18 June 1642
(University of Oxford, OU Archives, NEP/supra/Reg. Q, f. 200v).

The content of the tuition towards the BA degree varied with the tutor and to a lesser extent with the College to which the student belonged. Grammar was a major subject and studied from the works of Priscianus and Linacre. Rhetoric was studied from Aristotle, Cicero, Quintilian, and Hermogenes, whilst logic was read from Porphyry and Aristotle. Aristotle was the most important source for instruction in the above mentioned subjects and also politics, economics, and ethics. Greek and Latin were obviously the basis of all the instruction.

The above account is taken from the University Statutes but the various Colleges would have their own statutes and prescribed studies. These other subjects might include Mathematics, Astronomy, and possibly Science. Thus Willis in his four years at Christ Church would be thoroughly instructed in the classics, whilst studying the authors mentioned above, but might also gain some knowledge of science and even medicine.

On 12 June 1639, Willis graduated bachelor of arts, and after three more years of lectures and disputations, proceeded, on 18 June 1642, to the degree of master of arts. His subsequent career might have been in the church, and possibly to high office, but history intervened. Eleven days before Willis's MA, on 1 June 1642, Parliament delivered the Nineteen Propositions to the King, and the rejection of these by Charles led to the beginning of the Civil War in the summer of 1642.[6]

Consequently, Willis's further studies were at first interrupted by his service in the King's forces in Oxford and then diverted to medicine, when his king was captured and executed, to be replaced by a puritan protectorate, which proceeded to make prominent changes in Royalist Oxford. John Fell described this change in direction of Willis's career as follows:

> . . . the Church being trampled on, and Divinity together with the Divines suppressed, he applied himself to the study of Physik, in which, in a short time he made eminent progress.

So it transpired that Willis's medical studies coincided with the Civil War in Oxford.

REFERENCES

[1] Sir Charles Symonds and W Feindel. Birthplace of Thomas Willis, *British Medical Journal*, 1969, Vol 3, pp 648-9.

[2] Personal communication from Mr KH Rogers, Wiltshire County Archivist.

[3] D Swaye. *The Story of North Hinksey*. North Hinksey: Published by the Author, 1973.

[4] P Allen. Medical education in 17th century England, *Journal of the History of Medicine and Allied Sciences*, 1946, Vol 1, pp 115-43.

[5] HM Sinclair and AHT Robb-Smith. *A Short History of Anatomical Teaching in Oxford*. Oxford: Oxford University Press, 1950.

[6] FJ Varley. The Siege of Oxford. *An Account of Oxford During the Civil War*, 1642-1646. Oxford University Press, 1932.

Chapter 3

Willis's Medical Education in Oxford

I did attend the armed troops of Mars, Instead of Books I Sword,
Horse, Pistols bought, and on the Field I for Degrees then fought
An Undergraduate at Oxford University during the Civil War[1]

The seventeenth century medical training in the University of Oxford has been the subject of research in some detail.[2-4] Here we shall describe the tuition as defined in the statutes, before indicating the regime of study undergone by Willis. For this period in the history of Oxford University we are indebted to the contemporary commentary by Anthony Wood.[5]

Since the Medical Act of 1511/2, Oxford and Cambridge had played a central but not exclusive role in seventeenth century medical training and qualifications. Most physicians of any standing had a medical degree from one of these two universities, and a few, who wished to make sure of their credentials, qualified at both universities. Although it was possible to gain a medical degree by royal command, and the Archbishop of Canterbury could award a medical degree, as he still may, the regular procedure for an ambitious doctor was to gain a medical degree from Oxford or Cambridge. Whilst the qualification was essential, tuition at Oxford and Cambridge was not necessary, and many preferred that available on the continent. For the student pursuing his medical studies entirely at Oxford, a period of 14 years was required, and, shortly before Willis came to the University, the existing statutes were revised, although very few changes were made. Charles I had commanded William Laud, the Archbishop of Canterbury, to examine University education, particularly that at Oxford. The commission headed by Laud created revised statutes,which came into effect at Oxford in 1636, and were called the Caroline Code. That part referring to medicine will now be described.

Medical tuition was in the hands of the Regius Professor of Medicine, who was directed to lecture:

'in Hippocrates or Galen' to all students in medicine and bachelors [of medicine] until they [were] promoted to the doctor's degree in that faculty, or completed in the University the time required for promotion to the doctor's degree

The lecturer had to lecture for a *'full three-quarters of an hour, in his own person'*. The professor must not deliver his lecture hurriedly and at its conclusion he had to answer *'with kindness'* any arguments, questions, or doubts raised by his hearers. The student had to take a written record of the lecture, and if he were absent a fine of some pence was levied for non-attendance. The professor of medicine was also fined if he did not deliver the lecture.

By the time Willis came to the medical course, there were four offices in the teaching of medicine. The Regius Professorship, attached to Christ Church, had been founded by Henry VIII in 1546, and he was assisted by the Superior and Inferior Linacre Lecturers in Medicine attached to Merton College. A recent foundation in 1624 of the Tomlins Lectureship in Anatomy, was evidence of the modern importance of the subject, the study of which was assisted by the 1636 charter granted by Charles I, by which the Tomlins Reader could command the body of anyone executed within 21 miles of Oxford. The statutes of this new lectureship, which was occupied by the Regius Professor, were most detailed.[6] Every Spring, after the Lent Assizes, a '*Sounde*' body of one of the executed persons was demonstrated by the Reader, the dissection being performed by a '*Chirugian*'. In addition to the lectures and anatomical dissections, the medical student had to take part in two public disputations before he attained his degree of Bachelor of Medicine. Four more years of lectures were required for the doctorate, before which the candidate himself had to give six one-hour lectures on Galen.

The 14 years to the doctorate were made up of four to the BA, three more for the MA, three for the BM, and four more for the DM. This prolonged period of study leading to a thorough knowledge of the works of Galen and some knowledge of anatomy was not often pursued. It was more common to study in Europe at Paris, Leiden, Padua, Basel, or Montpellier, and on return ask for an Oxford degree. Those students who chose to remain in Oxford were dilatory in attendances, despite the fines. Attendance was poor at lectures and worse at disputations. Sometimes classes could not be held as not a single student was present.

Willis's attendance to his medical studies was quite exceptional for its brevity. He began his medical studies after he qualified MA in June 1642, the same month in which the Civil War began, and he graduated BM in December 1646, a few months after the city of Oxford was surrendered by the Royalists to Fairfax. During the years of the Civil War in Oxford, all university instruction, including that of medicine would have been constantly disturbed. The first episode of the war in Oxford was a brief occupation of the city by the Parliamentary forces, during which time, Willis wisely left the city. In a few days Lord Saye and Sele's troops left Oxford which on 29 October welcomed the King in these fulsome words uttered by the University rather than the City: 'Our Oxford... stands clear, gilded by the beams of Your Majesty's royal presence'. Willis returned to Oxford to resume his studies. Oxford became full of Royalist troops, a major component of whom were new formations raised from the University dons and students, the 'town' being less enthusiastic with the call to arms. Willis himself, encouraged by his Regius Professor of Medicine, enlisted in an auxiliary regiment raised from members of the University by the Earl of Dover. Fellows and scholars alike had to assist in the digging of trenches and the construction of fortifications. In addition to the soldiers of the Army, the King, Queen, and Court descended on Oxford, and occupied many of the Colleges causing further disruption. As a result of the overcrowding in Oxford, and the conditions in the military encampments around Oxford, there were several serious epidemics of fever, in one of which Willis's father died. Laxity in conduct amongst the billets in Oxford caused several fires, one of which caused a great deal of damage to the city. The state of Oxford during the Civil War will be further described in the next chapter. Suffice it here to emphasise that Willis spent little time listening to the customary readings from Hippocrates and Galen.

The current Regius Professor of Medicine, Thomas Clayton (1575-1647), had been, for his time, an excellent occupant of that post, but now, long in years, and preoccupied with the royalist cause, as befitted a Regius Professor, his days of medical instruction were over. He also had other duties, combining with his professorial chair the Tomlins Readership of Anatomy, and being the last Principal of Broadgates Hall and the first Master of the newly founded Pembroke College. Thomas Clayton died in 1647, and was succeeded by his son, who became Sir Thomas Clayton (1612-1693). Sir Thomas Clayton was probably the worst occupant of the Oxford Regius Chair of Medicine in all its history, devoting most of his time to self-advancement, to such effect that he became Member of Parliament for the University in 1660, Warden of Merton (1661-1693), and was knighted by Charles II. Anthony Wood describes him as 'being posses'd with a timorous and effeminate Humour, could never endure the sight of a mangled or bloody Body'. The supervision of the dissections required in teaching anatomy were quite beyond his state of mind and, having at first used William Petty as a deputy, he resigned the Tomlins Readership to Petty in 1650, the most distinguished act of his career. Thus Willis was fortunate in having the gifted Petty as his teacher in medicine and anatomy for a few years after the Civil War, and until Petty left Oxford in 1651. Willis and Petty were of the same age, became good friends, and spent much time together. They both achieved fame in the revival of Anne Green in Petty's lodging in 1650.

The Civil War effectively ended with the defeat of Rupert's Royalist Army by Fairfax at the Battle of Naseby on 14 June 1646, the remainder of the conflict being the besieging of towns held by Royalists. Charles I had left Oxford secretly on 27 April and, on 24 June, Sir Thomas Glenham had surrendered Oxford to Fairfax.

Willis concluded his formal medical education on 8 December 1646, when he was awarded the degree of Bachelor of Medicine, four and a half years after his degree of Master of Arts. These years, coincidental with the Civil War, had been exciting for the Country and for Oxford, but scarcely conducive to study. It is unlikely that Willis attended many lectures and these remnants of a classical medical education were probably abandoned in the troubled times. Willis may have been lucky in being spared three years of Hippocrates and Galen. Instead he had, by chance as a medical student in the royalist forces, personal experience of illnesses such as the camp fever, to which his father succumbed.

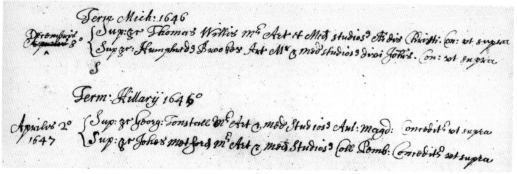

Record of Willis's Bachelor of Medicine degree, conferred on 8 December 1646
(University of Oxford, OU Archives, NEP/supra/Reg. Q, f. 73r).

However, my reading of Willis's upright character and thorough classical schooling leads me to suggest that Willis would have done his best, alone or with such instruction as he could find, to study the customary medical education in the University of Oxford. His award of the BM was, however, due to the recommendations of Thomas Clayton, the Regius Professor, who neglecting to teach his medical students could scarcely refuse to support them to their degrees.

Nevertheless, Willis was fortunate in being granted his degree in December 1646 and being able to begin medical practice as a qualified, albeit untrained, doctor. Soon the triumphant rebels would be arriving in Oxford. They would punish the Royalists, fill the positions in the University with their nominees, and try to convert the University of Oxford to their Protestant ways. Cromwell himself would become Chancellor of the University. Therefore, Willis might not have received his BM degree if Thomas Clayton had not swiftly rewarded him for his loyal army service to the King.

REFERENCES

1   CE Mallet. *A History of the University of Oxford*. London: Methuen, 1924-7. Chapter XVIII of Vol 2 deals with the Civil War.
2   A Chaplin. A History of Medical Education in the Universities of Oxford and Cambridge, 1500-1850, *Proceedings of the Royal Society of Medicine*, 1920, Vol 13 (section on the history of medicine), pp 83-107.
3   P Allen. Medical education in Seventeenth century England, *Journal of the History of Medicine and Allied Sciences* 1946, Vol 1, 115-43.
4   HB Sinclair and AHT Robb-Smith. *A Short History of Anatomical Teaching in Oxford*. Oxford: Oxford University Press, 1950.
5   A Wood. *Athenae Oxoniensis: An Exact History of all the Writers and Bishops Who have had their Education in the University of Oxford*, new edn, Philip Bliss, 4 Vols. London: Rivington, 1813-1820.
6   HM Sinclair. Oxford medicine. In: *Medicine in Seventeenth Century England*, Edited by Allen G. Debus. Berkeley, Los Angeles, London: University of California Press, 1974.

Chapter 4

The Civil War, the Protectorate and Commonwealth, and the Restoration. The Medical and Scientific Community around Willis in Oxford

The period of spectacular scientific advance coincided with the economic, political and religious changes of the Puritan Revolution

Charles Webster[1]

In June 1642, at the age of 21 years, Willis graduated MA, thus completing his general education first as a schoolboy at Sylvester's Academy in the High, and subsequently as an undergraduate at the college of Christ Church, in the University of Oxford. He remained in Oxford for a further 25 years, moving to London in 1667. This quarter century of his life in Oxford was crammed with achievements. In these productive years he chose his profession of medicine, acquired a self-taught proficiency as a doctor, and practised his medical skills with such assiduity that his fame survives today. His medical practice was so remunerative that, before his removal to London, his income was the highest in Oxford. Coincidentally with Willis's career in Oxford there were striking changes in that city, and also throughout England, and to a lesser extent in Scotland and Ireland, many of them related to the Civil War. A brief account of the Rebellion, the succeeding Protectorate and Commonwealth Period, and the subsequent Restoration will give this important background to Willis's work, and career, which was first arrested, then changed and obstructed, and finally accelerated. This period of the Civil War in Oxford has been extensively researched.[2-5]

The Grand Remonstrance presented to King Charles by his Long Parliament on 1 December 1641 marked a climax in the expression to the King of the discontent of his subjects with his conduct of affairs in England, Scotland, and Ireland. The King's fruitless attempt to arrest the five members of the House of Commons precipitated the Civil War. He was compelled to leave London to rally his forces which faced the Parliamentarians at the battle of Edgehill on 23 October 1642. Edgehill was indecisive and on 29 October Charles and his troops entered Oxford, which became the King's capital throughout the War.[2,6,7] Anthony Wood records the words of welcome by the University as 'Our Oxford stands clear, gilded by the beams of Your Majesty's royal presence'. This was the natural reaction of the Anglican Churchmen, who predominated in the University. It is doubtful if the citizens were as enthusiastic. They had just bidden farewell to the Parliamentarians under Lord Saye and Sele, who left on

20 September, having 'taken' Oxford on 14 September, an occupation of the city during which Willis left Oxford.

The King and his forces left Oxford on 3 November, marching and taking Benson, Henley, and Reading but, losing confidence, turned back from an assault on London, and returned to Oxford on 29 November. From this day, Oxford became the base of the King, not only for his military operations, but for his Court, Mint, Exchequer, and such government that the circumstances permitted to him. Thus New College became the powder magazine, Thomas Bushnell set up the Royal Mint in New Inn Hall, and a Royalist Parliament met in Christ Church Hall. Roundhead prisoners were held in St Michael's church.

The total dislocation of Willis's medical studies was described in Chapter 3. Here we shall only describe those events which led to a change in Willis's career. He wished, according to John Fell, to become an Anglican clergyman. He was diverted to medicine, because of the dislocation of the University, and the death, in June 1643, of his father, and 10 days later his stepmother, both deaths being due to 'camp fever', arising from the epidemics in the troops of both sides of the conflict. This left Willis as the eldest and 'in charge' of two conjoined families living in two farms in North Hinksey and South Hinksey, two villages lying between Royalist Oxford and Abingdon, now occupied by the Roundheads. He may also have been moved by the epidemics of fever he observed and he also remembered assisting Mrs Iles, wife of a canon of Christ Church, who 'was a knowing woman in physic and surgery, and did many cures'.

The Protectorate began a new era for Oxford, interesting and important, and characterised by such profound changes in Oxford University, as to constitute an academic revolution.[8] The Battle of Naseby on 14 June 1645 ended the first Civil War and any credible hopes of a military victory for the King, who had left Oxford secretly on 27 April 1646. Oxford ceased to be a Royalist stronghold on 24 June 1646, when Sir Thomas Glenham surrendered the City to General Fairfax. The Royalist troops marched amicably over Magdalen bridge through the Parliamentary lines to an encampment on Shotover Hill. The subsequent military exploits of the King and the short second Civil War were ultimately fruitless and in 1649 his trial was swiftly followed by his execution on 30 January.

The victorious Parliamentary forces and the subsequent Protectorate immediately began the conversion of Royalist Oxford to a puritan city and University. They were incensed at the part the city had played in the Civil War but also wished to control the first University in the land and the major centre for Anglican churchmanship. They began with directives which were largely ignored by the Heads of the Oxford colleges and their fellows. However, in October 1646 a censorship of the Oxford University Press virtually ceased its printing operations. Samuel Fell, Dean of Christ Church, and Vice Chancellor was the leader of the Oxford resistance against its new masters. Inevitably sterner measures were directed against Oxford in the form of visitations to compel the Royalist dons to change their ways or to be expelled from their positions. In May 1647 the Parliamentary Visitors for Oxford were named and they had power to enquire whether members of the university had failed to take the Covenant and the Negative Oath, had opposed the Parliamentary ordinances or had fought against the Parliamentary forces. The Visitors met at Merton, and commanded the attendance of the Vice Chancellor, the Heads of Houses, and the Fellows. The university responded with a passive resistance but with little compliance. Most dons attended, as requested, but enquired by what authority the Visitors could overturn their statutes, and their former oaths to the King. The Visitors eventually prevailed and the dons either submitted or were removed from their offices. Many Heads of Houses were ejected, Bayle from St John's, Radcliffe from Brasenose, Potter from Trinity, and Oliver from Magdalen. The most important ejections were of Gilbert Sheldon from All Souls and Samuel Fell from Christ Church. The saga of the forcible removal of Mrs Fell and her family from the Deanery of Christ Church is told elsewhere. Willis from his rooms in Peckwater may have seen the removal of the Fell family, amongst them Mary, his future wife. Dr Iles, Willis's original patron at Christ Church, lost his position as a canon, to which he never returned. Willis himself remained in his rooms in Christ Church. Perhaps with timidity he took the oaths required or, more likely, not being a Fellow of a college, and pursuing medicine rather than divinity, he was not asked to appear before the Visitors. Obviously he was not under close observation, or the authorities were indulgent, for in his rooms in Christ Church, and subsequently in his house, Beam Hall, he and his Anglican friends attended church services using the forbidden church liturgy.

The total upheaval of the senior university positions in Oxford brought in new appointees, chosen by the puritans, to occupy the vacancies in the colleges and halls. Many of them were conspicuously more modern and innovative than those they succeeded. In 1646 there were some 25 colleges and halls making up the University of Oxford. Of these six, Christ Church, Wadham, Merton, All Souls, Queens, and Trinity were important in the 'explosion' of scientific talent which gathered in Oxford during the Protectorate. We may understand the abrupt personnel changes in Oxford by reviewing those in these six colleges.

Christ Church required a new Dean when the redoubtable Samuel Fell was forcibly removed and imprisoned, and Edward Reynolds, one of the Parliamentary Visitors became Dean from 1648-1651. Reynolds proved an able and competent Dean but was eclipsed by his successor from 1651-1659, John Owen (1616-1683), a puritan divine, who became Vice Chancellor, and was prominent in beginning the cataloguing of the Bodleian Library. He attended Sylvester's school, as did Willis and the new head of Wadham, the brilliant

John Wilkins (1614-1672) who succeeded the ejected Warden, Pitt. Merton had lost its Warden, Harvey, who was replaced by Jonathan Goddard (1616-1675), Cromwell's physician from 1651-1660. Goddard was a physician interested in anatomy, chemistry, and optics, and on leaving Merton became Professor of Medicine at Gresham's College, London. All Souls had lost Gilbert Sheldon who was succeeded by the physician, John Palmer, and the college subsequently admitted Thomas Sydenham and Christopher Wren to fellowships. At Queens, Langbaine had placated the Visitors and survived as Provost, but was replaced by Thomas Barlow (1607-1691) from 1657-1675. Barlow was a clergyman, had been Bodley's librarian, and was a close friend of Robert Boyle and John Owen. Trinity lost its president Hannibal Potter, who was replaced by the ageing Robert Harris, a puritan divine, and one of the Parliamentary Visitors. On the death of Harris in 1658, after a year of the sick William Hawes, Seth Ward was made President to be replaced at the Restoration by the ageing Potter. Ralph Bathurst was a prominent fellow at Trinity, submitted to the Visitors, and survived in his fellowship, to become President himself for 40 years, a most productive period for Trinity.

The above account is concerned only with the heads of six Oxford colleges but many Fellows were removed and replaced with others acceptable to the puritans, and some of these new dons were important in medicine and science (see Chapter 6 which will deal with Willis's friends, colleagues, and acquaintances).

The death of Oliver Cromwell on 3 September 1658 presaged the end of the Commonwealth and Protectorate period which extended from 1649-1660. The succession of Richard Cromwell was short lived and the country called for the restoration of the monarchy, in which movement, in Oxford, the Vice Chancellor, Conant and the Dean of Christ Church, Reynolds, were active. On 10 May 1660 Oxford proclaimed the restoration of Charles II, and a hogshead of claret was put into Carfax Conduit to run in its east and south pipes.[9] In September 1663, King Charles II made a protracted visit to Oxford to receive the acclamation of the City and its university.

Oxford University again experienced sweeping changes as the Puritans in the University were displaced by the Royalists, a reversal effected with less difficulty as the mood of Oxford was, on this occasion, supportive. Reynolds had to vacate the Deanship of Christ Church, and after a few months of Morley, John Fell became Dean. Oliver came back to Magdalen, Sheldon to All Souls, Bayle to St John's, Potter to Trinity, Newlyn to Corpus, Mansell to Jesus, Wightwick to Pembroke, and Walker to University. Mallet has given details of these and many other changes at this time in the heads and fellows of the colleges of the University.[8]

The upheaval in the life of Willis will be described in Chapters 5 and 6. With the restoration Willis entered his most productive period, and his tenure of the Sedleian chair of Natural Philosophy is described in Chapter 5. Robert G Frank Jr, has thoroughly researched this period in Oxford,[10] and has composed a delightful account of an imaginary stroll through Oxford in the late spring of 1659, two years after Willis had married Mary and moved into Beam Hall, opposite Merton chapel. With permission, I reproduce this passage.

All good walking-tours of Oxford begin at Christ Church; ours should be no exception. Owen presides over a vast and rich college whose common room includes Nathaniel Hodges, John Ward, Robert Lovell, Richard Lower, Robert Hooke, Henry Stubbe, John Locke, and more than a dozen lesser philosophers and medical men. A few minutes' walk takes us across Christ Church's great quadrangle, through Peckwater, and out by way of Canterbury quad, where Willis had his rooms, into Oriel Square. Looking east 120 yards or so down St John Street (now Merton Street), we can see Merton, where Dickenson has his laboratory and Richard Lydall, his rooms. Richard Trevor is on leave studying medicine in Padua, but Goddard might possibly be in the Warden's lodgings on one of his periodic visits. On the north side of St John Street, opposite Merton is Beam Hall. There Thomas Willis lives and practices with his younger associates, such as Lower, and maintains the chemical laboratory in which Hooke served his apprenticeship.

A few minutes' walk north on Oriel Street brings us to the High Street, in the centre of intellectual and scientific Oxford. Twenty-five yards to our left, on the south side of the High, is Buckley Hall, where Harvey's apothecary, John Clarke, had his shop, and where the 'clubb' met in Petty's lodgings on the second floor; Matthew Wren lived in the same building. In the next block, also on the south side, are the bookshops of Richard Davis and Thomas Robinson. But we turn right, to the east, and walk along the south side of the High Street the hundred yards to Arthur Tillyard's, where we check his coffee room for friends. A few steps takes us past the Three Tuns to Deep Hall. Here, opposite John Palmer's lodgings, John Crosse has his apothecary shop and, more importantly, Robert Boyle his lodgings. If we had arrived in late 1659, we might have seen Peter Stahl setting up to give classes in chemistry. As it is, there is no meeting of the club today, and Boyle, Hooke, and Daniel Cox are conducting experiments with the vacuum pump.

If we were to continue for a quarter of a mile down the High Street, we would come to the Physic Garden, where Jacob Bobart presides and gives instruction in botany to medical students such as John Ward. Across the street from him is Magdalen College, where Petty's Tomlins deputy, Henry Clerke, has a fellowship. Joshua Crosse, the Sedleian Professor, lives nearby; Bobart is his next door neighbour.

But we decide to cross the High and enter All Souls. Millington, Castle, and Pett are in their rooms, as is Christopher Wren, who is the college Bursar. Things are unsettled in London, and Wren is not reading his lectures there as Gresham Professor of Astronomy. Leaving All Souls and walking the 150 yards up Cat Street to the Schools Quadrangle, we pass John Wallis's house, and then on our right, Hart Hall, where the Principal, Philip Stephens, is giving his anatomy class. Peeking up New College Lane, we can see the college of the same name, where Boyle's friend Robert Sharrock is writing up his experiments on plants as Boyle suggested he do. Sharrock will soon be editing Boyle's *New experiments Physico-mechanicall Touching the Spring of Air* for publication by Thomas Robinson.

It is early afternoon as we enter the Schools, so there are no lectures or disputations. Tacked on the door are notices announcing the times and places of the lectures Millington and Hodges will read for DM degrees. To the east and south are the scientific schools. Natural Philosophy is in the far left corner on the first floor, and directly above it is the Anatomy School with its collection of bones and and exotic specimens. Mornings, Seth Ward reads in the Astronomy School on the second floor to the right, behind us, while Wallis lectures in the sister room on the same floor to our left. Immediately ahead of us is the entrance to Bodley's great library, where Stubbe is the Under-Librarian.

Leaving the Schools, we walk the few hundred yards up to Wadham. Wilkins is still Warden, although he will soon resign to become Master of Trinity College, Cambridge, and has recently been spending much time out of town. Seth Ward is in residence; his friend Ralph Bathurst will exercise his good offices to have Ward elected into the vacant presidency of Trinity. Some of the scientists who have lived in Wadham are gone: Lawrence Rooke to London, Francis Crosse to study medicine at Leyden, Charles Morton to a parish living in Cornwall, and William Neile to his country estate at White Waltham in nearby Berkshire. But there are still a number of virtuosi, such as the fellows Thomas Spratt and Walter Pope, in residence. Thomas Jeamson is a scholar there, and John Mayow and Thomas Guidott are still undergraduates. Mayow will soon be elected scholar, a position he will hold only briefly before going on to a fellowship at All Souls.

The last few hundred yards West through the garden brings us to Trinity, where Ralph Bathurst is senior fellow. His good friend and fellow chemist, John Lydall, has been dead for two years, and some of the virtuosi who made the college an attraction for Harvey—men such as Nathaniel Highmore and George Bathurst—are also gone. The scientific tradition at Trinity has long since merged with other circles.

We have walked slightly more than two-thirds of a mile, and it has been less than half an hour since we left Christ Church gate. For the scientists in midcentury Oxford, it was a small town indeed.

The quarter century of Willis's maturity in Oxford stands as a golden period of scientific enlightenment in England. If one tries to picture the bearers of the torch of scientific discovery, it must be conceded that several of these bearers, amongst them Willis, were in Oxford during these 25 years.

REFERENCES

1 C Webster. *The Great Instauration: Science, Medicine and Reform 1626-1660*. London: Duckworth, 1975.
2 CH Firth. A chronological summary of the Civil War in Oxfordshire, Buckinghamshire and Berkshire 1642-1646. In: *Proceedings and Excursions of the Oxford Architectural and Historical Society* (new series), 1890, Vol 36, pp 280-91.
3 FJ Varley. *The Siege of Oxford*. Oxford, 1932.
4 A Carter and J Stevenson. *The Oxfordshire Area in the Civil War*, 1974.
5 M Toynbee and P Young. *Strangers in Oxford*. London: Chichester, 1973.
6 A Wood. *The Life and Times of Anthony Wood, Antiquary, of Oxford, 1631-1695, Described by Himself*, edited by A. Clark, 5 Vols. Oxford: Clarendon Press, 1891-1900.
7 CV Wedgewood. *The King's War 1641-7*. 1958.
8 CE Mallet. *A History of the University of Oxford*, Vol 2. London: Methuen, 1924. Reprinted 1968.
9 JM Falkner. *A History of Oxfordshire*. Oxford, 1899.
10 Robert G Frank Jr. *Harvey and the Oxford Physiologists*, Berkeley, Los Angeles, and London: University of California Press, 1980.

Chapter 5

Willis's Medical Career in Oxford

... he applied himself to the study of Physick, in which, in a short time he made eminent progress

John Fell, 1675

Willis began his medical practice in Oxford in 1647. He was qualified, having received his degree of bachelor of medicine on 8 December 1646, but untrained, since, as we have seen in Chapter 3, his period of medical studies coincided with the Civil War.

He proceeded to establish a medical practice from his rooms in Christ Church, as would be possible for a doctor in Oxford with a medical degree, and a former student of the College. His patients at first would not be drawn from Oxford, as these would be cared for by established doctors in Oxford. What Willis did was customary for a novice medical practitioner. He visited the markets in the small towns around Oxford and stood there offering his services to the general public. We know from John Aubrey that Willis visited these markets and in particular that held at Abingdon. William Petty left Oxford towards the end of 1651, and commented that Willis was still visiting Abingdon market and 'casting waters'. This phrase describes the custom of doctors of prescribing treatment based on an examination of a patient's urine. The convenience of this was that the urine specimen could be brought to the market by a relative or friend by whom the prescription or medicament could be sent back to the patient. Today this type of medical practice seems absurd. Urinalysis was, however, the only form of clinical investigation in general use and was the precursor of today's extensive clinical tests. The point also to be noted is how, in this way, Willis began his own study of the urine of his patients. Later he was to discover the difference between the polyuria of diabetes mellitus and that of chronic kidney disease. The sweetness of the urine in diabetics, enabling the doctor to distinguish this particular disease from other causes of polyuria, was of fundamental importance, and this discovery had its foundations in Willis's early experience at the markets.

To visit the markets in the small towns around Oxford required transport. Willis at first, to lessen the expense, shared ownership of his horse with Richard Lydall (1621-1704) another struggling medical practitioner of the same age as Willis. Qualified doctors such as Willis and Lydall were competing with many practitioners, who had no recognised qualifications. These quacks prescribed not only medicines but charms and other magical procedures to cure ailments. Willis complained that a third of his patients had previously received treatment from these unlicensed practitioners whose remedies he described as 'a sword in a blind man's hand'. Their remedies were indeed bizarre but so also were those of Willis. The difference was that Willis and his medical contemporaries were dedicated to a search for remedies with a rational basis and therein lay the seeds of the modern scientific study and treatment of disease.

Willis's practice was at first very small and he would have leisure for many other pursuits. Always industrious, Willis used some of his time in scientific research in his rooms in Christ Church. We know this from John Aubrey's reference to Willis who 'studied chymistry in Peckewater Inne chamber'. Richard Lower and Robert Hooke participated in these researches in Christ Church. Willis also was a prominent member of the group meeting at Wadham College, who, according to Seth Ward, 'have joyned together for the furnishing an elaboratory'. John Evelyn described the facilities provided by John Wilkins at Wadham to include telescopes, furnaces, beehives, laboratories, and other apparatus in Wilkin's rooms and in the spacious grounds of the College.[1] There were several other places of scientific excitement: Boyle's lodgings in John Crosse's house in the High, Petty's rooms, called Bulkley Hall, and the apothecary's premises of Arthur Tilliard, both close by the High. For the group of scientists assembling in Oxford, there was much to do at a time when physics, chemistry, biochemistry, physiology, and animal experimentation were subjects in their infancy, and anatomy was in need of monumental revision. Boyle's experiments with respiration, experiments on the circulation of the blood, the transfusion into animals of blood and other liquids or drugs in solution, and the use of the microscope by Hooke, and later by Wilkins and Wren are notable examples of ongoing scientific research, then beginning in Oxford. Peter Stahl from Strassburg was invited to Oxford by Boyle and gave lectures in chemistry. Necropsies were frequently performed by for example, William Conyers (1622-1665) whose post-mortem examinations were seen and recorded by Anthony Wood and John Ward. This period of scientific research in Oxford has been thoroughly examined and elegantly described by Robert G Frank Jr.[2]

On 14 December 1650, Willis and William Petty became famous for a strange incident of resuscitation.[3-5] The subject of their intervention was Anne Green (or Anne Greene) who was seduced by the son of the great house where she worked, became pregnant and gave birth to a child, probably stillborn, which she concealed. Her crime discovered, she appeared before the magistrate, Serjeant Upton Croke, was found guilty of murder, sentenced to death, and duly hanged on the gallows in Oxford. She hung for a half hour during which time her relatives swung on her legs to effect an end to her sufferings. She was pronounced dead, placed in a coffin, and taken to Bulkley Hall, the lodgings of William Petty, for anatomical dissection. Petty, the Tomlins Reader in Anatomy, arrived with Willis to carry out the dissection. The coffin had been opened and an onlooker, hearing the corpse breathe, was trying, by stamping on her chest,

Bulkley Hall, lodgings of William Petty. From an engraving by J. Skelton dated 1821.

to end her life. Willis and Petty proceeded to revive her, to such good effect, that she made a complete recovery, became famous, was pardoned, married in Steeple Barton, and bore three children. This unusual patient brought fame to Petty and Willis, which when Petty moved from Oxford and left medicine, devolved entirely on Willis, and materially helped his medical reputation. Willis also succeeded the gifted Petty as the leading medical scientist in Oxford.

By 1657 Willis's medical practice and financial resources allowed him to marry and he moved with his new wife into Beam Hall. During the years that followed, he built up a substantial clinical practice and conducted his extensive research in anatomy and other scientific subjects. His facilities for his medical and scientific work in Oxford are of considerable interest. He also journeyed far into the country to see the rich in their houses on their country estates.

Beam Hall was of adequate size for a successful practitioner, and on moving there from his rooms in Christ Church, Willis again set up a laboratory. In Beam Hall, Willis employed three servants and his coachman, Thomas Bush. Willis saw patients there but also dispensed medicines, an important part of seventeenth century medicine, and the basis of financial success. Willis made sure of this by devising his own recipes and by having them manufactured by his own pharmacist, John Hemmings, a resident in his house. As his practice grew, Willis acquired other premises. He went into partnership with two more senior doctors, Dr Peter Elliot (1618-1682) a physician practising in the High, and an Oxford surgeon, Mr William Day (1604-1665). The three doctors leased and renovated the Angel, a dilapidated old coaching house on the High near Magdalen bridge.[6] The Angel, near the important bridge crossing the Thames, was situated on an essential thoroughfare for travellers from the North and West of England to London, and so was an ideal location for attracting medical practice from the rich coaching travellers. Communications with London were continually improving and a few years hence, on 26 April 1669 the 'Flying

Beam Hall (also spelt Biham Hall), on the left, and Postmasters Hall,
on the right, in an eighteenth century print.

Beam Hall, today (Mr Dudley).

Coach' would begin its service, leaving Oxford at 6 am and reaching London at 7 pm, omitting the usual overnight stop at Beaconsfield. The Angel was used for consultations but also for medical treatments. It had, according to John Ward, an excellent 'fluxing chair'.[7] Some patients would stay there with nursing care so the establishment was in effect a small hospital. When Mr Day died, Willis and Dr Elliot leased the property called Bostar Hall, at numbers 86 and 87 of the High.[8] The late Kenneth Dewhurst studied this capitalist venture of Willis and has illustrated the south side of the High as it would appear in seventeenth century Oxford.[9] From Magdalen bridge, we first see the Angel, then numbers 86 and 87, formerly Bostar Hall, then Dr Elliot's house, then after the intervening University College, Boyle's house and laboratory, and finally the house and premises of Arthur Tilliard, the apothecary. This is a remarkable collection of near or adjacent buildings devoted to medicine, and a foretaste of the concentration later seen in Harley Street, London. It also helps to explain the considerable financial success of Willis, who was probably the leading partner in the enterprise.

We now come to a most important change in Willis's professional life, which was a direct consequence of the restoration of the monarchy. Many Oxford dons lost their positions amongst them, in 1648, Joshua Crosse, the Professor of Natural Philosophy, to which chair Willis succeeded in 1660.[10] Joshua Crosse, originally a Fellow of Lincoln, was a supporter of the Presbyterians, and had been intruded into a Fellowship at Magdalen, the office of Senior Proctor, and the Sedleian Chair of Natural Philosophy. In the Sedleian chair, Crosse had replaced the ejected Royalist, John Edwards, and now was himself ejected, it was stated on the charge of embezzlement. Fortunately for science, Willis was appointed, mainly on the instigation of Gilbert Sheldon, who had been reinstated as Warden of All Souls.

There had been three previous Sedleian Professors of Natural Philosophy, Edward Lapworth, and the two mentioned above, Edwards and Crosse. The chair, established belatedly from provision in the will of Sir William Sedley in 1618, was intended to promote the study of Aristotle. The writings of Anthony Wood[11] and the University Statutes[12,13] have given us the responsibilities of the chair as summarised here. The professor must read in full term, on Wednesdays and Saturdays at 8 am, from the books of Aristotle, either *Physics, de Coelo et Mundo, de Meteoris, Parva Naturalia, de Anima, or Generation and Corruption.* His audience was composed of the bachelors of arts, who were also the auditors in astronomy, and who were fined some pence for non-attendance. Willis would have been fined 10 shillings if a lecture was not given.

Science gained by the scant heed Willis gave to the statutes. Although the restoration had brought back to Oxford many academics, who were of the Aristotelian tradition, and many of them in his college of Christ Church, Willis determined to champion the new Baconian Philosophy. He devised a series of lectures on subjects such as 'the Offices of the Senses' and 'the Faculties and Affections of the Soul'. The earlier series of lectures included what he termed the 'received Opinions of others' but later series began to incorporate his own theories and original data from his researches. Anatomy and particularly the anatomy of the nervous system began to be included as a major component. These lectures changed as Willis incorporated new teaching material based on his researches; consequently they were up to date and popular, attracting a far wider audience than the readings from Aristotle. The record of John Locke, who attended these lectures, has preserved the form of the series of lectures in the year 1661 or 1662, and their alteration, incorporating new material, in the academic year 1663/1664.[9] These lectures formed the basis of Willis's textbooks.

The importance of this Sedleian chair to the career of Willis deserves emphasis. Without it, Willis would have been a successful physician, making discoveries in medicine and science, but possibly not sharing his findings and theories by publication. The diligent Willis, on accepting the obligations of the chair, constructed a series of lectures, which brought to his attention the imperfections of knowledge of his subjects. He then set about performing experiments and dissections to improve his knowledge, which he then incorporated into his lectures, and later published. The bequest of Sir William Sedley in 1618, which created the chair had an effect on science and medicine, in this one professor, quite beyond its monetary value. Three hundred years later, Lord Nuffield was to see a similar multiplication of his gifts when he endowed the Nuffield chairs in Oxford.

Willis's first book, *Diatribae Duae Medico-Philosophicae*, in 1659 gave many of his early remedies and founded Willis's reputation as an iatrochemist, Paracelsian, or Helmontian. Some disciples considered themselves Willisians. His recipes for the 'unlocking' of iron and sulphur were not fully divulged, and were coveted by physicians and apothecaries. Willis was criticised by the Royal College of Physicians for keeping this remedy secret, and it seems many people wanted the recipe. JR Partington was of the opinion that this remedy was 'syropus diasulphuris prepared from sulphur of wine mixed with canary wine, sugar, and elder flowers'.[14,15] Willis was innovative in his remedies, seeking, from the new subject of chemistry, drugs active in illnesses. There were few to be found amongst the simple chemicals then discovered, and Willis's pharmacopoeia included, perforce, many strange herbal and animal concoctions. Willis was interested in the healing properties of famous springs such as Bath and Tunbridge Wells. He would analyse the water chemically, to determine the salts present. One day in 1664, riding through Astrop, near King's Sutton, in company with Richard Lower, they discovered, by the chance of the thirst of Willis's horse, a spring whose water seemed the equal of other famous spas. This finding, his subsequent analysis of the water, and the good opinion of some of his patients, gave Willis a reputation for the judgement of water from medicinal springs. Several years later in London he was asked to examine other spring water for the Royal Society.

The medical practice of Willis grew prodigiously, partly from his incessant industry, but also from the efficient organisation of his work. His income was now the highest of any person residing in Oxford. Tenure with Dr Eliot of about half of the properties on the North side of the High considerably enlarged his medical practice, which began to include many persons residing in London. Willis had reached a plateau of work in the small city of Oxford. London, the capital, with the Royal College of Physicians, and the Royal Society, now had many excellent doctors and scientists, several from his own circle in Oxford and some his own students. Many of his old friends, and not only in medicine, were in London, including Christopher Wren and Robert Boyle who were now prominent in the capital. His move to London in 1667 was a natural extension of his career, although the precipitating factor was the persuasive invitation to Westminster by his old patron, Gilbert Sheldon, now Archbishop of Canterbury.

REFERENCES

1   *The Diaries of John Evelyn*, Vol 3, edited by ES de Beer. Oxford: 1954, pp 110-11.
2   RG Frank Jr. *Harvey and the Oxford Physiologists*. Berkeley, Los Angeles, London: University of California Press, 1980.
3   Richard Watkins, *Newes from the Dead. Or a true and Exact Narration of the Miraculous deliverance of Anne Greene*. Oxford, 1651.
4   *The Petty Papers*, Vol 2, edited by the Marquis of Lansdowne. London: 1927, pp 157-67.
5   Robert Plot, *The Natural History of Oxfordshire*. Oxford, 1677. Reprinted 1972.
6   *Oxford City Documents (Financial and Judicial)*, Vol III, edited by JE Thorold Rogers. Oxford, 1891, p 343.
7   John Ward, *Diary*, 16 Vols. Washington DC: Folger Shakespeare Library.
8   Oxford tradesmen's tokens, edited by HE Salter. In: *Surveys and Tokens*. Oxford: ET Leeds, 1923.
9   K Dewhurst. *Thomas Willis's Oxford Lectures*. Oxford: Sandford Publications, 1980.
10 Oxford University Archives. *Convocation Register 1659-1671*.
11 A Wood. *The History and Antiquities of the Colleges and Halls of the University of Oxford*, edited by John Gutch. Oxford: Clarendon Press, 1756.
12 *Oxford University Statutes*, translated by GRM Ward. Oxford: Clarendon Press, 1845.
13 *Statutes of the University of Oxford Codified in the Year 1636 Under the Authority of Archbishop Laud*, edited by John Griffiths. Oxford: Clarendon Press, 1888.
14 JR Partington. *A History of Chemistry*, Vol 1, London, 1965.

Chapter 6

Willis's Friends, Teachers, Colleagues, and Pupils

*In the midst of those distractions, which then miserably rent
the public affairs, Oxford was remarkably distinguished by a
confluence of learned men of all parties and persuasions*

Anthony Wood (1632-1695)

Willis had few teachers, but many friends, colleagues, and pupils. He also had
many acquaintances in England and abroad. The consideration of all these
contacts requires some order. His close family will be described in Chapter 12.
Here we will deal with his teachers, his important Oxford contemporaries, his
contacts during the last nine years of his life spent in London, his acquaintances
elsewhere in England, and his correspondents abroad. Details of the lives of
many of these persons can be found in standard biographies to which reference
is made.[1] Further references are made to more comprehensive biographies and to
works in which a link with Willis is given. Many personal details will be found
in the contemporary writings of Anthony Wood,[2,3] and a few in the diaries of
John Evelyn[4] and John Ward,[5] and in the writings of John Aubrey[6] and Robert
Boyle.[7] The archives of the University of Oxford[8] provide evidence of the status
and activities of individuals in the University.

These various persons will be grouped under the headings of: his close personal
friends, his teachers, his close medical colleagues in Oxford, his other medical
and scientific colleagues in Oxford, his colleagues in London and elsewhere in
Britain, and his contemporaries abroad.

Close personal friends

Willis's close personal friends, outside his medical and scientific work, included
Richard Allestree, John Dolben, John Fell, and Gilbert Sheldon, all divines,
whose lifelong friendship with Willis began during the troubles they shared
during the civil war and the protectorate. He was also a neighbour of Anthony
Wood.

Richard Allestree (1619-1681) entered Christ Church in 1636, two years
before Willis, having been educated at the Free School, Coventry. He took his
BA degree in 1640 but soon after joined the Royalist forces under Sir John
Biron. A close friend of Willis, he was present at Willis's wedding in April 1657.
Allestree suffered greatly under the Protectorate but the Restoration reversed his
fortune. He was made a canon of Christ Church and in 1665 Provost of Eton
College. Not only was he a distinguished scholar but also an able administrator
contributing greatly to the restoration of the fortunes of Christ Church, where

Oil painting in Christ Church by Sir Peter Lely (1618-1680) of three lifelong friends of Willis. John Fell (afterwards Dean of Christ Church and Bishop of Oxford) on the left, John Dolben (afterwards Archbishop of York) in the centre, and Richard Allestry (afterwards Provost of Eton) on the right (Governing Body, Christ Church, Oxford, LP Cat no. 74).

he was treasurer, and of Eton, both institutions having suffered during the disturbances of the Civil War. A relative was James Allestry a bookseller in London who printed several of Willis's books but was ruined by the Great Fire of London. Richard Allestree is buried in the chapel of Eton College.

John Dolben (1625-1686) came from Westminster School to Christ Church in 1640, two years after Willis. His undergraduate studies were seriously disturbed by the Civil War, in which he took an active part on the side of the King. Marching north with the Royalist Army he fought and was wounded at the Battle of Marston Moor, then helped to defend York, besieged by Fairfax. At the close of the Civil War, Dolben returned to Christ Church, took his MA, but was removed from the College by the Parliamentary Visitation of 1648. In 1656, now ordained, he married the niece of Gilbert Sheldon, and stayed in St Aldates with his father-in-law, Richard Sheldon. The following year he participated at the wedding of Willis. During this time he came to the regular services at the home of Willis at Beam Hall. Dolben became Dean of Westminster in 1662 and Archbishop of York in 1683. He died in 1686 and is buried in York Minster.

John Fell (1625-1686), brother of Mary, became a lifelong friend of Willis. They were students together at University, although Willis was older by four years. Their great friendship probably began in the civil war when, during the siege of Oxford, both served in the same regiment, raised by the Earl of Dover. A closer bond arose during the Protectorate, when, deprived of his position in Christ Church, and in the Anglican Church, John Fell may have stayed with Willis and his sister in their house, Beam Hall. Fell was the leading churchman of the group of dispossessed divines, and later spoke of his gratitude to Willis for his bravery at a difficult time for the Anglican Church.

With the Restoration, the fortunes of John Fell changed. He became Dean of Christ Church, as had been his father, and in 1676 he was appointed Bishop of Oxford. His Deanship at Christ Church is memorable for his restoration of its buildings and encouragement of poor scholars and general improvement of academic standards. Today he is also remembered for the verses of Thomas Brown (1663-1704) beginning 'I do not love thee, Dr Fell'. In this biography, the obituary of Willis by John Fell has proved useful in providing several statements about Willis's life and family.

It is appropriate here to note the attendances of Allestree, Dolben, and Fell at the services first at the lodgings of Willis in Christ Church, and later at his house in Beam Hall. These three were removed from their positions in Christ Church, because they refused to submit to the Parliamentary Visitors. Possibly Willis did submit, or not being in holy orders his compliance was not insisted upon, and when he married and lived in Beam Hall, he was not a member of the University. The period of these and many other guests of Willis is remembered in the Anglican church, when the services and sacraments of the proscribed church of England were maintained in defiance of the law. The enforcement of the puritan prohibitions was probably lax in Oxford, since even after the efforts of the Visitors, the majority of the University would have been sympathetic to the old services. With the Restoration, the wheel turned full circle, and Allestree, Dolben, and Fell were rapidly elevated. They all became canons of Christ Church in July 1660 and, on 3 October of the same year all three were given the degree of Doctor of Divinity.

Gilbert Sheldon (1598-1677) was of a generation earlier than Willis but is included here since successive steps of Willis's career were directly due to his patronage. Sheldon came to Trinity College, Oxford, in 1614, from which he graduated BA in 1617 and MA in 1620, being ordained in 1622. Becoming a Fellow of All Souls in 1622 and Warden in 1626, he was, during the Protectorate, a determined opponent of the Parliamentary Visitors, suffering ejection from his Wardenship and imprisonment. His loyalty to the executed Charles I and in exile to the future Charles II brought great rewards following the Restoration. He was reinstated as Warden of All Souls in 1659, became Bishop of London in

1660, and Archbishop of Canterbury in 1663. Sheldon had great influence with the new king who recommended Willis for the degree of Doctor of Medicine. The appointment of Willis to the Sedleian chair of Natural Philosophy was made by Sheldon, who later encouraged Willis's remunerative move to London. Thus many major steps in Willis's career were directly attributable to the patronage of Sheldon to whom Willis dedicated several of his books.

A final comment on these three close friends of Willis, and Sheldon, an older patron, gives insight into Willis's character, his choice of friends in his undergraduate days, and those with whom he chose to remain associated throughout his life. Including as they did, Archbishops of Canterbury and York, the Provost of Eton, and the Dean of Christ Church, they form a remarkable group. Willis, himself an example of piety and strict adherence to the Anglican Church, was happy in the company of its most illustrious office bearers. A memorial to these three contemporary friends of Willis exists in Christ Church in the form of a painting of the three divines executed by Sir Peter Lely (see p 35).

Willis's teachers

There is little evidence of Willis's formal teaching in medicine, and this paucity of recognisable mentors is evidence of the dislocation of studies in Oxford throughout the civil war. Four persons deserve mention, William Harvey, Thomas Clayton, William Petty, and Robert Boyle, and of these, probably only Petty exerted a direct influence on Willis's studies in medicine.

William Harvey (1578-1657)[9-10] came to Caius College, Cambridge, from King's School, Canterbury. He gained his Cambridge degree in 1597, after which he studied medicine in Padua, graduating there and also in Cambridge in 1609. He settled into medical practice in London, being appointed physician to St Bartholomew's Hospital. In 1628 he published his famous *De Motu Cordis*. He was successively physician to James I and Charles I, and was present with Charles at the Battle of Edgehill. He resided in Oxford with the King during the Civil War, and was nominally Warden of Merton College from 1645-1646, more to give him a base in Oxford near the King than as a permanent position as head of Merton. Probably Willis saw very little of Harvey, but he must have been influenced by his presence in Oxford, and Harvey's books would have been familiar. Harvey had wide interests, including scientific subjects remote from medicine. He advocated the experimental approach to the solution of problems in physiology and he recommended autopsies for the understanding of diseases.

Thomas Clayton (1575-1647)[11] was Regius Professor of Medicine in Oxford from the time Willis came to Oxford to the time (1646) he was awarded his BM. The Regius Professor, or his deputy, was the main source of instruction

William Harvey, present in Oxford during the Civil War, and 'mentor' to Willis
(Hope Collection, Ashmolean Museum, University of Oxford).

in medicine, and his statuary duties were to read Hippocrates and Galen twice weekly. Clayton became Regius Professor in 1611 in succession to his father-in-law, Anthony Aylward. In 1617 the Mastership of Ewelme was added to his chair and in 1624 the Regius Professor also became the Tomlin's Reader in Anatomy. Clayton was an important figure in Oxford, having been the last principal of Broadgates Hall, and becoming the first Master of Pembroke College. For the time, he was an excellent physician, anatomist, and teacher, but Willis probably gained little instruction from him, as the last years of his professorship coincided with the Civil War. Whilst academic instruction was in abeyance, Willis was otherwise known to Clayton, who raised the University Legion, a body of 600 University students under arms, to fight for the King in Oxford. Willis enlisted for the King, no doubt his absence from his studies was condoned, and his loyalty repaid later by the award of his medical degree.

William Petty (1623-1687)[12] was 2 years younger than Willis, but by chance was in some measure Willis's teacher. Petty was a gifted child whose natural genius had flourished from an unconventional education. He went to sea, was abandoned in France, which misfortune he turned to advantage by being educated at the Jesuit College at Caen. Returning to England, he joined the Royal Navy, but the Civil War decided him to return to the continent, where he studied medical subjects at Utrecht and Amsterdam. He graduated in medicine

William Petty, Tomlins Reader in Anatomy in Oxford, and medical colleague of Willis in Oxford (Hope Collections, Ashmolean Museum, University of Oxford).

at Leyden in 1644, then went to Paris where he became a friend of Hobbes. He came to Oxford in 1646 and from 1648 to 1657 was the deputy of Sir Thomas Clayton (1612-1693) as the Regius Professor of Medicine and Tomlins Reader in Anatomy. Sir Thomas was the son of the previously mentioned Thomas Clayton, and an inferior successor as a doctor and anatomist. Clayton junior was 'possest with a timorous and effeminate humour, could never endure the sight of a mangled or bloody body', and his wisest act was to appoint the gifted young Petty as his deputy. Petty gained his Oxford DM in 1650 and in the same year was given a fellowship at Brasenose College. His knowledge of science, anatomy, and medicine had benefited by his studies and travels on the continent. Being of a similar age to Willis, Petty was a natural companion and it is likely that Willis's interest and aptitude for anatomy came from this influence. Petty and Willis gained fame from their revival of Anne Green in 1650. Unfortunately for Oxford, Petty soon went to Ireland as Physician-General to Cromwell's army but then was given the much greater task of the surveying and mapping of the whole of Ireland.

Robert Boyle (1627-1691) the seventh, youngest, and favourite son of Richard Boyle, the first Earl of Cork, was educated at Eton, then privately on

Robert Boyle, scientific colleague of Willis in Oxford
(Hope Collection, Ashmolean Museum, University of Oxford).

the continent, touring France, Switzerland, and Italy for some six years. He attained that supreme education in languages, arts, and sciences then available to a rich young man. He settled in Oxford from 1664-1668. Six years younger than Willis he came to Oxford after Willis had begun his medical practice but before he was Sedleian Professor. Boyle came to Oxford at the invitation of John Wilkins, set up his own private laboratory, where began his science which led him to his ultimate status as the foremost scientist of the seventeenth century.

Close medical colleagues in Oxford

Willis's close associates in his research work were Ralph Bathurst, Thomas Millington, Christopher Wren, and Richard Lower, all of whom contributed to his first major work, the *Cerebri Anatome*.

Ralph Bathurst (1620-1704), a year older than Willis was a school fellow of Allestree at the Free School, Coventry. He came to Trinity College where he took his MA in 1638, became a fellow in 1640 and was president from 1664, combining this office with the Deanship of Wells. Bathurst's inclinations were always to the church, being ordained in 1644, but during the civil war, like Willis, he took up medicine. He qualified MD in 1654 and practised in Oxford, initially alongside Willis at Abingdon market. Sprat describes Bathurst as the 'principal and most constant attender' at the scientific meetings at the lodgings of Dr Wilkins in Wadham College, one of the forerunners of the Royal Society. In medicine he was the daily companion of Willis, both in medical practice and in medical science. He is said to have helped revise the text of *Cerebri Anatome* and possibly written the preface. On the Restoration Bathurst resumed his clerical career becoming the Dean of Wells, but refusing other preferments that might detract from his main work as head of Trinity College.

Ralph Bathurst, close medical colleague of Willis in Oxford
(Hope Collection, Ashmolean Museum, University of Oxford).

*Thomas Millington, medical colleague of Willis in Oxford
(Hope Collection, Ashmolean Museum, University of Oxford).*

Thomas Millington (1628-1704) was educated at Westminster School, and, after his MA at Trinity College, Cambridge in 1657, moved to Oxford, took his MD, and became a Fellow of All Souls. He succeeded Willis as Professor of Natural Philosophy and subsequently was successful as a London Physician, being President of the Royal College of Physicians. He was an important member of Willis's medical and scientific team, apparently contributing to many discussions. Willis in *Cerebri Anatome* describes Millington as 'most Learned Man, to whom I from day to day proposed privately my Conjectures and Observations, often confirmed by his Suffrage, being uncertain in mind, and not trusting to my own opinion'.

Christopher Wren (1632-1723) came to Wadham College from Westminster School, graduating BA in 1651, proceeded MA and was elected a Fellow of All Souls in 1661. In 1657 he was made professor of astronomy at Gresham College and in 1661 returned to Oxford to the Savilian chair of Astronomy. Wren was an important member of Willis's 'research group', inventing methods to further the anatomical work and contributing several drawings to *Cerebri Anatome*.

*Christopher Wren, who drew several of the pictures in Cerebri Anatome for Willis
(Hope Collection, Ashmolean Museum, University of Oxford).*

Richard Lower (1631-1691) was Willis's junior by 10 years. Educated at Westminster School, he came to Christ Church in 1649, graduated MA in 1655, and MB and MD in 1665. A successful physician and early anatomist and physiologist, his chief fame is that of carrying out the first successful blood transfusion from the veins of one animal to another. Lower's medical studies in Oxford came after the disturbances of the Civil War and the Protectorate, and coincided with Willis's most productive period around his appointment as Sedleian Professor in 1660. Lower did many of the dissections for the text of *Cerebri Anatome* and some of the drawings are his. Willis gave due credit for this assistance and Lower remained a firm friend of Willis, defending the writings of his revered teacher on the subject of fevers from a vitriolic attack by a Bristol Physician, Dr E O'Meara, described by Lower as *'a little frog from the swamps of Ireland'*.

Richard Lower, pupil of Willis (Hope Collection, Ashmolean Museum, University of Oxford).

Other medical and scientific colleagues in Oxford

Willis's medical practice in Oxford brought him into contact with several helpers and colleagues in his work. We have mentioned that Ralph Bathurst was a fellow practitioner, sharing the 'open air' practice at Abingdon market. Richard Lydall (1621-1704) was also an early medical colleague, with whom at first, Willis shared the expense of his horse. Later when Willis's practice at his home, Beam Hall, in Merton Street, had become large, Willis employed an apothecary, John Hemmings. Later the expansion of his practice required more space and, with Dr Peter Elliot (1618-1682) and a surgeon, Mr William Day (1604-1665), he leased and put in order an old coaching inn in the High, called *The Angel*. Two other figures deserve brief mention. John Locke (1632-1704), a student of Willis, became a considerable physician and experimental scientist, in addition to his greater fame as a philosopher. Anthony Wood (1632-1695) an antiquary and biographer attended Merton College from 1647-1652, after which he lived in Postmaster's Hall adjacent to Willis. Wood's writings are the most important contemporary source of information concerning Willis, and have been described in the biographical foreword of this work. Wood knew Willis well and attended his lectures.

The remaining doctors and scientists in Oxford to be considered include members of a large group of researchers in science and medicine. Robert G Frank Jr has examined this group as scientific descendants of William Harvey and I am indebted to his book[13] for many details recorded here. Frank's researches have identified over 110 individuals in Oxford interested and active in the new scientific subjects, and this figure does not include physicians who were currently graduating in Oxford. A measure of the scientific activity is the numbers of books produced in this golden age at Oxford when more than 580 books were produced, of which 240 were important to science, medicine, and technology.

Further evidence of the seminal importance to science of Oxford in the second half of the seventeenth century is the foundation of the Royal Society. The constitution of a group at Wadham College and another at Trinity College at this particular time has been the subject of extensive historical research arising from claims and counterclaims concerning the origins of the Royal Society. These various groups were called by a variety of names such as 'The Invisible College', 'The Virtuosi', and the 'Oxford Experimental Clubbe'. It is now recognised that there were several groups of scientists in London and in Oxford at this time and some researchers at differing times would be members of several societies. What is important in a biography of Willis is that Oxford was particularly active at this time in science and that Willis was a prominent member of these groups. Looking at Oxford in the seventeenth century, it is convenient to group scientists according to the College to which they belonged, since they usually met and worked in a particular College. Many were Fellows of a college, in which they resided. Wadham, Merton, Christ Church, Trinity and All Souls were all colleges with several scientists, and have been arranged here in order of approximate numerical strength in science. Some names appear in two college lists.

Wadham College (14) was then a new foundation and its partiality to science is directly attributable to its Warden, John Wilkins (1614-1672).[14] For a small college of recent foundation Wadham was unusually well represented in science by Christopher Brookes (?-1665), Francis Crosse (1631-1675), Thomas Guidott (1638-c1703), Thomas Jeamson (1638-1674), George Joyliffe (1621-1658), John Mayow (1641-1678), Charles Morton (1627-1698), William Neile (1637-1670), Samuel Parker (1640-1688), Walter Pope (c 1627-1714), Lawrence

John Locke, pupil of Willis. His 'notebook' is a record of Willis's series of lectures as Professor of Natural Philosophy (Hope Collection, Ashmolean Museum, University of Oxford).

Rooke (1622-1662), Thomas Sprat (1635-1713), Seth Ward (1617-1689), and Christopher Wren (1632-1723).

Merton (12), with Harvey briefly as Warden, had Edward Browne (1644-1708), William Coles (1626-1662), Edmund Dickenson (1624-1707), Jonathan Goddard (1616-1675), Edward Greaves (1608-1680), John Greaves (1602-1652), Richard Lydall (1621-1704), Henry Munday (1623-1682), Charles Scarburgh (1616-1694), Richard Trevor (c 1628-1676), Daniel Whistler (c 1619-1684), and Robert Wood (c 1622-1685).

Anthony Wood, biographer and neighbour of Willis
(Hope Collection, Ashmolean Museum, University of Oxford).

Christ Church (11), large in buildings and with many students would naturally have many researchers. Willis himself was of this college, in which he lived and did his earliest research. Other members of Christ Church were Richard Allestree (1619-1667), Nathaniel Hodges (1629-c 1655), Robert Hooke (1635-c 1651), John Locke (1632-c 1652), Robert Lovell (1630-c 1655), Richard Lower (1631-c 1691), John Masters (1637-c 1665), John Owen (1616-c 1630), Henry Stubbe (1632-1656), Francis Vernon (c 1637-1658), and John Ward (1629-1648).

Trinity (18) another small college attracted scientists and persons interested in science and these included John Aubrey (1626-1697), George Bathurst

(1610-1645), Ralph Bathurst (1620-1704), Philip Fell (1633-1682), Nathaniel Highmore (1613-1685), John Lydall (1623-1657), Samuel Parker (1640-1688), and Daniel Whistler (c 1619-1684).

All Souls (6), with Gilbert Sheldon as Warden, was prominent in science as is evident from the list below, some of whom moved to All Souls from other Colleges. George Castle (c 1635-1673), Philip Fell (1633-1682), John Mayow (1641-1679), Thomas Millington (1628-1704), Peter Pett (1630-1699), and Christopher Wren (1632-1723).

No other colleges in Oxford attracted so many students or researchers. Of the important scientists, not mentioned above, Walter Charleton (1620-1707) was at Magdalen Hall (also John Wilkins' first place of study), William Petty was educated abroad and received a fellowship at Brasenose, and John Wallis (1616-1703) was educated at Exeter College. Some scientists with private means chose to work in Oxford but not in immediate contact with the University. Robert Boyle (1627-1691) set up his private laboratory at 88 High Street, and Walter Needham (c 1631-1691) conducted his scientific work privately in Oxford, having been educated in Trinity College, Cambridge. With these few exceptions all the major scientists in Oxford in this interesting period were connected with the colleges of Wadham, Christ Church, Merton, Trinity and All Souls. This is an interesting localisation of scholarship at the University level, and the previous formative years of these students at school is of interest. Westminster School from its link with Christ Church sent several students whose names appear amongst the scientists above. Frank[10] has researched the pre-eminence of Westminster School at this particular time.

Colleagues in London and elsewhere in Britain

Many of Willis's friends and colleagues in London were known to him from an earlier period in Oxford. Boyle, Charleton, Harvey, Hooke, Lower, Needham, Petty, and Wren all completed their careers in London, as did Willis himself. Outside Oxford and London, Francis Glisson, Sir Thomas Browne, and Thomas Sydenham require mention. For this London period of Willis's life, reference may be made to the papers of the Royal College of Physicians[15,16] and those of the Royal Society.[17]

Francis Glisson (1597-1677), a graduate of Cambridge where he was Regius Professor of Physic for 40 years, was a considerable figure in anatomy, physiology, and pathology, being a founder of the Royal Society. He was an excellent physician becoming president of the Royal College of Physicians, and is credited with the first clear description of infantile rickets.

Sir Thomas Browne (1605-1682) was educated at Winchester College and at Broadgate Hall (which became Pembroke College), Oxford. His extensive and broad education continued with travels in Ireland, France and Italy. He studied medicine additionally in Montpellier and Padua, graduating as a doctor of medicine at Leyden and Oxford. Six years older than Willis, he had settled in Norwich in 1637, where he remained undisturbed by the Civil War, being knighted by Charles II in 1671. Medicine was only one of his interests, for in addition to a large medical practice, he wrote many literary works, highly praised by Charles Lamb, and Thomas De Quincey, and maintained a voluminous correspondence with his many friends in England and abroad. Willis makes frequent mention of Browne's medical practice.

Thomas Sydenham (1624-1689)[18] came from Dorset in 1643 to Magdalen Hall, Oxford at the age of 17, when Willis, three years older, had already taken his MA and begun his medical studies. Sydenham left Oxford after a few months to join his family fighting in the Parliamentary forces in that part of the Civil War proceeding near their home. He returned to Oxford in 1647, read medicine at Wadham, and graduated MB in 1648, becoming a fellow of All Souls. He obtained his Oxford MD in 1676 but was never elected a fellow of the Royal College of Physicians. Distinguished for clinical observation, he published many important works which cannot be detailed here. These two doctors knew each other well. Sydenham, in many ways was the opposite of Willis, not favouring necropsies or animal experimentation.

Willis's contemporaries abroad

As far as we know, Willis did not venture outside England, and did not meet any of his contemporaries in science and medicine living on the continent. Little of his correspondence has survived but there is evidence in his own writings of his knowledge of work relevant to his own. What follows is a brief mention of important figures abroad whose work would be known to Willis, more details being available elsewhere.[19]

Jean Baptiste van Helmont (1577-1644), a Capuchin friar who turned to medicine, was an important disciple of Paracelsus. Helmont made important observations on gases, ferments, bile, and gastric juices. Willis derived many of his ideas from this source and from Franciscus de la Boe, or Sylvius (1614-1672), a Leyden professor and pupil of Helmont. Willis's interest in chemistry and its place in therapy was in direct succession to Paracelsus, Helmont and Sylvius.

Willis seems to have used microscopy very little but must have known of the work of Athanasius Kircher (1602-1680), a Jesuit priest of Fulda, who first turned the microscope on human diseases. The low magnification he used makes it unlikely that his 'worms' were organisms. The superior optical performance of the microscopes of Antonj van Leeuwenhoek (1632-1723) of Delft, permitted a sight of large bacteria. The work of both these microscopists was added to greatly by that of Robert Hooke (1635-1703), a pupil of Willis and Boyle. Before the principles of disease caused by organisms could be established, the fallacy of spontaneous generation had to be demonstrated. This was achieved by Francesco Redi (1626-1694), an Italian naturalist of Arezzo, who by exposing meat under controlled conditions, demonstrated that maggots would only appear if access to flies was permitted.

The *De Homine* of René Descartes (1596-1650), an early textbook of physiology would have been known to Willis, and Descartes' *Des Passions de l'Ame* published in 1649 with the first experiments in human reflex action might have encouraged Willis's thoughts on neural reflexes. Anatomists would have a direct influence on Willis's work and his on theirs. The work of Jan de Wale (1604-1649) supported that of Harvey, and important anatomical discoveries were being made by Thomas Bartolinus (1616-1680), Marcello Malpighi (1628-1694), and Jan Swammerdam (1637-1680). Raymond Vieussens (1641-1716), of Montpellier, followed Willis and specialised in the study of the anatomy of the nervous system, and also made important observations on the anatomy of the heart and the internal ear. With the anatomist, Niels Stensen (1648-1686), an admirer but also a critic of Willis, we must close this brief review of some of Willis's contemporaries abroad.

REFERENCES

1   Dictionary of National Biography. London: 1917.

2   Anthony Wood. *Athenae Oxoniensis: An Exact History of All the Writers and Bishops who have had their Education in the University of Oxford*, new edition, Philip Bliss, 4 Vols. London: Rivington, 1813-1820.

3   *The Life and Times of Anthony Wood, Antiquary, of Oxford, 1632-1695, Described by Himself*, edited by Andrew Clark, 5 Vols. Oxford: Clarendon Press, 1891-1900.

4   *The Diary of John Evelyn*, edited by ES de Beer. 5 Vols. Oxford: Clarendon Press, 1955.

5   John Ward. *Diary*. The original 16 manuscript Vols are held in the Folger Shakespeare Library, Washington DC.

6   *'Brief Lives', Chiefly of Contemporaries, Set Down by John Aubrey, Between the Years 1669 & 1696*, edited by Andrew Clark, 2 Vols. Oxford: Clarendon Press, 1898.

7   *The Works of the Honourable Robert Boyle*, edited by Thomas Birch, 2nd edn, 6 Vols. London: Rivington, 1772.

8   Joseph Foster, editor, *Alumni Oxoniensis: The Members of the Universities of Oxford, 1500-1714*, 4 Vols, Oxford, Parker, 1891-1892.

9   Sir Geoffrey Keynes, *The Life of William Harvey*. Oxford: Clarendon Press, 1978.

10   Robert G Frank Jr. *Harvey and the Oxford Physiologists*. Los Angeles: University of California Press, 1978.

11   HM Sinclair and AHT Robb-Smith. *A Short History of Anatomical Teaching in Oxford*. Oxford: Oxford University Press, 1950.

12 The Papers of Sir William Petty are now in the possession of his descendant, the Marquis of Lansdowne, and are kept at Bowood, Calne, Wiltshire.

13 Robert G Frank Jr. *Harvey and the Oxford Physiologists: A Study of Scientific Ideas*. Berkeley: University of California Press, 1980.

14 Barbara J Shapiro. *John Wilkins, 1614-1672*, Berkeley and Los Angeles: University of California Press, 1969.

15 William Munk, *Roll of the Royal College of Physicians of London*, 2nd edn, Vol 1. London: 1878.

16 *A History of the Royal College of Physicians of London*, by Sir George Clark, 2 Vols. Oxford: Clarendon Press, 1964-1966.

17 *The Correspondence of Henry Oldenburg*, edited and translated by A Rupert Hall and Marie Boas Hall. 11 Vols to date. Madison: University of Wisconsin Press, 1965.

18 K. Dewhurst *Dr Thomas Sydenham, (1624-1689): His Life and Original Writings*. Berkeley and Los Angeles, University of California Press, 1966.

19 *An Introduction to the History of Medicine*, 3rd edn, by FH Garrison. Philadelphia: Saunders, 1922.

Chapter 7

The Major Works of Willis

... he hath laid a lasting foundation of a body of physic chiefly on
hypotheses of his own framing
Anthony Wood (1632-1695)

The major works of Willis were published in seven separate books all in Latin, except for the last, which was published in English, in 1691, after the author's death. These seven published works conveniently encompass almost all of the medical and scientific observations and speculations of Willis. Here they are treated chronologically with comments on the details of their publication and their scientific content. The bibliography of Willis has been studied by HJR Wing,[1] to whom I am indebted for much of the information on the publication details.

Diatribae Duae Medico-Philosophicae (1659)

This, the first of Willis's major works, was first published in London in an octavo edition. *The Dictionary of National Biography* wrongly states that it was first published at The Hague. There is good evidence that the first printed copies were available in 1658. John Aubrey, the antiquary, purchased a copy from Allestry in 1658 and his copy is now in the Bodleian Library. On the flyleaf of this Bodleian copy, in Aubrey's handwriting, is a note that it was purchased for 3s 6d from Ja Allestry in 1658. Following this first edition, which it seems should be dated 1658/1659, there were three more editions in London, dated 1660, 1662, and 1677. The book was published at The Hague in 1662 and at Amsterdam in 1663 and 1669. Manget's *Bibliotheca Scriptorum Medicorum* Tomus II (1731) states there were editions at Amsterdam in 1665 and Leyden in 1680, copies of which were not seen by HJR Wing.

The title of '*Diatribae*' describes the work as consisting of two separate tracts, the first on Fermentation, and the second on Fevers, to which is appended a dissertation on Urine.

The tract on fermentation reveals much of Willis's speculations on the chemistry of organic processes. He drew on observations from his country life on a farm as well as his studies on the biology of animals and humans. The use of yeasts in the baking of bread, and in the fermentation of fruits and juices into wines and beers, their further change into vinegars, the fermentation of milk into butter and cheese, and the spoiling of food by decomposition were all subjects for his study. This work also contains his own theories of the chemistry underlying all biology. He considered all matter to be composed of varying proportions of five chemical principles. These were spirit, sulphur, and salt, which were the active principles, and water and earth, which were inert principles filling the space between the active principles. Fermentation was a process of change bringing some substances to perfection and others to spoliation. Fermentation was a process basic to the earth, and caused mineral springs, meteoric phenomena, and the atmospheric changes of the weather. To life it was fundamental since the 'fermentation' of the heart and the blood was essential, as was the fermentation in the stomach and intestines of the ingested food. Bile was produced by a fermentation in the liver and blood by fermentation in the spleen. Thus Willis was groping towards an understanding of the biological chemistry of the body, even to some concept of an endocrine system, since he considered that the fermentation of the sexual organs replenished the blood with a living ferment. Disease and finally death were due to some unwanted form of fermentation and methods of curing diseases could be based on the control of fermentation. As a skilled vintner creates good wine so the physician should control the ailments of the body by specific remedies. Excessive heat (fever) is managed by bleeding and measures to cause cooling. Alien matter in the body is removed by purgatives, emetics, and sudorifics. Weakness as in anaemia is strengthened by various nostrums of which iron was important.

The tract on fevers is of more lasting interest, as his analysis was based on many observed cases of febrile diseases. So many infantile, childhood, and adult diseases were then of an infectious nature that this study is remarkable for the perceived differences of febrile diseases when they were so numerous and all of unknown aetiology. Willis distinguished intermittent from continuous fevers and described how the intermissions could be quartan, tertian, and quotidian. These observations are the best evidence for malaria in England in the seventeenth century and in this treatise appears a detailed account of the use of 'that Peruvian bark', which was an early preparation of quinine. Willis noted that, unlike other antipyretics, quinine can suppress multiple paroxysms of fever, even if the treatment were given only on one occasion. Willis could hardly have known the explanation for the rational use of quinine, but he did realise its efficacy was exceptional, and predicted that more remedies with this efficacy would be discovered.

Willis recognised several types of fever. There were the continuous fevers, putrid fevers (presumably associated with purulent discharges), pestilential fevers, such as smallpox and the plague, lactation fevers associated with mastitis, and puerperal fever. His descriptions of epidemic fevers are of great interest, and Creighton considered Willis's account of three consecutive epidemics in 1657 and 1658 to be 'the first systematic piece of epidemiology written in England'.[2] Willis's description of *febris castrensis* (camp fever) is considered to be the first recognisable record of typhus fever in England. RH Major in his 'Classic Descriptions of Diseases' has reproduced Willis's *febris putrida* as an important early account of typhoid fever and his *febres pestilentes, ac malignae in specie* as typhus fever.[3] The modern literature of puerperal fever dates from Willis's account, which gave the clinical picture[4] and introduced the modern explanation of the condition.[5]

Cerebri Anatome (1664)

The *'Cerebri Anatome cui accessit Nervorum Descriptio et Usus'* was first published in London in a quarto edition in 1664, followed by an octavo edition in the same year. Several editions were printed in Amsterdam, one octavo in 1666, and duodecimo editions in 1664, 1667, 1676, and 1683, all reviewed by HJR Wing.

The work was dedicated to Dr Gilbert Sheldon, Archbishop of Canterbury and an important patron of Willis. The preface contained acknowledgements by Willis of the assistance of Dr Richard Lower, Dr Thomas Millington, and Dr Christopher Wren in the production of the book. These generous statements have led to the judgement that Willis was not primarily responsible and did not deserve the major credit for this important work, a belief fostered by Anthony Wood. This criticism has been adequately refuted, and for discussion on this point, the 1955 Harveian Oration of Sir Charles Symonds should be consulted.[6]

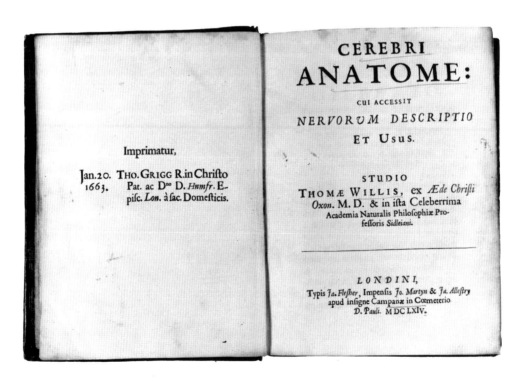

Title page of Cerebri Anatome, *1664 (Library of Christ Church, Oxford).*

This work on the anatomy of the nervous system, eclipsed all previous accounts, and remained the definitive textbook on the subject for about one and a half centuries. Its publication brought Willis enduring fame among the doctors and scientists of Europe as a modern anatomist of the first rank. The work consists of a practical treatise of the anatomy, not only of the brain, but of the spinal cord and also of the peripheral and autonomic nervous systems. It also abounds with numerous important original observations in neuroanatomy and neurophysiology. The contributions to science and medicine by Willis made in the publication of this textbook are detailed in Chapter 8.

Pathologiae Cerebri (1667)

The 'Pathologiae Cerebri et Nervosi Generis Specimen' was the succeeding work promised by Willis in the Cerebri Anatome and was first published in a quarto edition at Oxford in 1667. A duodecimo edition was printed in London by Allestry in 1668, and another in this size and in this year by Daniel Elzevir in Amsterdam. There was a further edition by Elzevir in 1670, and another edition, called the fourth, published at London. Although this was called a fourth edition, there is no trace of a third edition. At this time Allestry, Willis's original publisher, was in great trouble as his stock had been destroyed in the great fire of London.

Title page of Pathologiae Cerebri, 1667. *The engraving of Willis (which appears in the frontispiece), at the age of 45 years, signed* D. Loggan delin. et Sculp., *published in 1667, is the best likeness and the only surviving portrait of Willis executed during his lifetime (Library of Christ Church, Oxford).*

By now Willis was well known. This new work was reviewed in the *Philosophical Transactions* of the new Royal Society, and in the frontispiece of the book was a portrait of Willis engraved by Loggan. *Pathologiae Cerebri* is a very important work, which was well received by European doctors and scientists, and further enhanced the reputation of Willis. The work contains several crucial case reports describing diverse diseases some with the first ever recorded clear description.

His observations on convulsive disorders and on pathological conditions of the nervous system are of lasting significance, and are described more fully in Chapter 9. Here we shall mention that in this work the state of epilepsy was first defined as an entity separate from other neurological disorders. There is also in this work an excellent account of the clinical manifestations of asthma.

After the account of the convulsive disorders there is a confused account of scurvy, confused because, as Willis himself points out, many diverse and unrelated conditions–an 'immense medley of symptoms'–are included under the heading of scurvy. Willis seems to know that a diet of salted and smoked meat is conducive to scurvy whilst dairy products and fruit protect but he lacks conviction in his dietary recommendations.

Affectionum Quae Dicuntur Hystericae et Hypochondriacae (1670)

This work was first published in a quarto edition in London in 1670. Subsequently, there was a duodecimo edition at Leyden in 1671 and a third edition at London in 1678.

The work is in three parts dealing in turn with hysteria and hypochondria, blood, and muscular action. All are of considerable importance in the history of our understanding of these subjects.

Understanding of both hysteria and hypochondria was confused in Willis's day. In common with several contemporary physicians Willis rejected the notion that hysteria was caused by a displacement of the uterus, but also disagreed with Highmore that it was associated with pulmonary congestion. Willis was certain that the explanation of both these disorders was in the brain, which is probably his meaning of a convulsive disease. His ideas of treatment of hysteria and hypochondria now seem confused but his recommendation of iron probably relates to its efficacy in iron deficiency anaemia. He writes of 'green sickness', and possibly in his practice the condition of chlorosis was prevalent.

The second treatise concerned the action of the blood. This is an elaboration of Harvey's work, which Willis accepted entirely. He describes the oxidation of the blood in its passage through the lungs thus 'for what did flow of a dark purple colour into the Pneumonic Vessels from the right side of the Heart, returning from thence presently out of the Lungs, becomes crimson, and as it were of a flame-colour, and so shining, passes through the left Ventricle of the Heart and the appending Arteries'. There is much more on this subject combining his thoughts on the circulation of the blood and the way this disseminates metabolic energy products throughout the body.

The last part of this publication contains Willis's theories of muscle action, a scientific problem that was to remain unexplained for some centuries. Willis confused the function of the tendons with those of the muscles, and his idea that during rest the energy dwelt in the tendons to effervesce into the muscles during movement now seems absurd. However, he does mention his idea of reflex action, a notable point in the beginning of the literature of the neuro-muscular reflex.

De Anima Brutorum Quae Hominis Vitalis ac Sensitiva Est (1672)

The *De Anima Brutorum* was first published in a quarto edition in Oxford in 1672 and again in the same year in an octavo edition in London and Amsterdam. A further duodecimo edition appeared in Amsterdam in 1674. The many editions of this work provide evidence of its contemporary reputation. This book is one of the great works of medical science and was considered by Willis his most important publication. It was written in solitude after the tragic death of his wife 'that I might the less think on my grief'. The preface includes a tribute to Dr Edmund King and Dr John Masters for valuable assistance. Willis must have been very busy as he describes how he was 'being almost continually interrupted by my practice'. The work was dedicated to Dr Gilbert Sheldon, Archbishop of Canterbury, and to the Vice Chancellor, Doctors, and Masters of the University of Oxford.

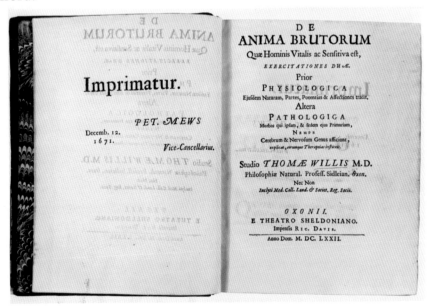

Title page of De Anima Brutorum, *1672 (Library of Christ Church, Oxford).*

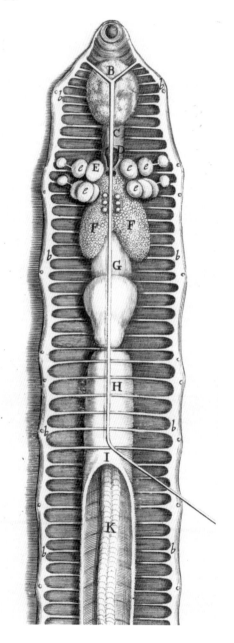

Dissection of an earthworm.
Drawing from De Anima Brutorum,
(Library of Christ Church, Oxford).

The book is divided into two parts, the first 'showing the nature, parts, powers, and affections of the soul', whilst the second deals with pathological states affecting the brain, 'unfolding the diseases which affect the soul and its primary seat, namely, the brain and nervous stock'. This book abounds with original observations. In comparative anatomy the reader will meet with very skilful and accurate dissections of the silkworm, oyster, lobster, and earthworm. In clinical medicine there are observations and speculations on the function of the brain and the manifestations of its disorder.

For example the sections dealing with sleep and subconscious states are thought-provoking as are Willis's theories on headache and vertigo. What however makes *De Anima Brutorum* of abiding importance is the first descriptions of certain clinical diseases and syndromes, of which two are so important that they alone could solely form the basis for the fame of Willis as a clinician. These two conditions are the state of *paracusis Willisii*, and the disease, *myasthenia gravis*.

Pharmaceutice Rationalis (1674-1675)

This work is in two parts, the first, published at Oxford in 1674, and the second part, usually bound separately, published, also at Oxford, posthumously in 1675. The first part was dedicated to the Royal College of Physicians of London, and in the preface Willis again makes acknowledgement to Drs King and Masters for their assistance. The whole work comprises a compilation of the 'materia medica' then available, but the recipes are interspersed with anatomical, physiological, and clinical observations and speculations. The preface to Part 1 gives an insight to the methodical way in which Willis thought and worked:

> the operations of Medicine are so many and various, I will treat of them in order according to the places where they first and chiefly begin to work; and first of Catharticks, or Cleansing Medicine, both Vomits and Purges: Next of Diuretics, or Medicines that provoke Urine, Diaphoreticks, or such as cause Sweating, and Cordials; and lastly of Opiates, or such as cause Sleep etc. and those that are commonly called Specificks, that is, such as are applied to the irregularities or defects of each particular Member or Entrail.

Thus we see how Willis thought of bodily systems, one of which might be deranged and susceptible to specific remedies. In describing diuretics Willis remarks on the sweet taste of the urine in diabetes, which he considers a disease of the blood rather than of the kidneys. His speculations on the cause of diabetes mellitus are however a nonsense by today's standards. At the end of this first part Willis deprecates the smoking of tobacco and the drinking of coffee.

The second part of *Pharmaceutice Rationalis* is dated 12 November 1675, the day after the death of Willis. It was dedicated to the University of Oxford, and also contained the postscript added by Dr John Fell, in memory of Willis. The work dealt with the 'places of Operation in our Bodies . . . that the true and real Hypotheses of Diseases shall be built, whereof we have designed the remedies'.

The use of the microscope is described in the preface. The anatomy of the lungs and the respiratory tract are described and illustrated, and then their illness considered, followed by the remedies suggested. Again in this publication, we find evidence of the originality of Willis as a clinician, for there is here a convincing account of the disease whooping cough, which he calls 'Chin-Cough'. Having dealt with respiratory diseases Willis then turns to the 'lower belly', considering its diseases and their possible remedies. The last part of this work deals with the efficacy and effects of bleeding as a therapeutical procedure, and finally some remarks on diseases of the skin and their treatment.

A Plain and Easie Method of Preserving Those That are Well From the Plague (1691)

This work first appeared as an octavo edition in London in 1691, 16 years after the death of Willis. It was a compilation edited from the manuscripts of Willis mostly written about 1666 and contains a number of prescriptions. It is the only major work of Willis to be published in English, and is of lesser importance than the preceding six works, being probably not intended by Willis for publication. J Hemming, Willis's apothecary edited this work, taking advantage of many of Willis's papers in his possession. The Royal College of Physicians of London approved of this publication, which was commended by the President and Censors on the 5 September 1690.

Of the seven books listed above, three, the *Cerebri Anatome*, the *Pathologiae Cerebri*, and the *De Anima Brutorum* are of the greatest importance in the development of our understanding of anatomy, physiology, and of our recognition of distinct human diseases. They form an interesting trilogy, planned in this form by Willis, of which the first dealt with the anatomy of the brain, the second with the pathology of the brain, whilst the last is concerned with the soul or psyche. This master plan was augmented in these three works by the addition of observations and conjectures on many allied subjects, additions which also grace all his works. The present author, familiar with modern clinical cases, finds the case reports taken from Willis's busy clinical practice to be the most valuable of all Willis's work. Willis's anatomical and physiological discoveries have had to be corrected and amplified over the years but his accurate case reports will remain a mine of information on clinical observation in the seventeenth century.

REFERENCES

1   HJR Wing. *A Bibliography of Dr Thomas Willis (1621-1675)*. Thesis submitted to the University of London, 1962.
2   C Creighton. *A History of Epidemics in Britain*, Cambridge: Cambridge University Press, 1891. Reprinted by London: Frank Cass, 1965.
3   RH Major. *Classic Descriptions of Disease*. Springfield, Illinois, 1955.
4   EH Ackerknecht. *Kurze Geschichte der Medizin*. Stuttgart, 1959.
5   CH Peckham. A brief history of puerperal infection, *Bulletin of The Institute of the History of Medicine*, 1935, Vol 3, p 192.
6   C Symonds. The Circle of Willis, *British Medical Journal*, 1955, Vol 91, pp 119-124.

Chapter 8

Willis's Contribution to Neuroanatomy and Neurophysiology

'The First Inventor of the Nervous System'
Heinrich Boruttau[1]
' The Harvey of the Nervous System'
Russell Brain[2]

The two quotations show that Willis's contribution to the understanding of the structure and function of the nervous system can scarcely be exaggerated. The magnitude and significance of his anatomical studies and physiological deductions may be appreciated by a comparison of the subject before and after his lifetime. Before the time of Willis, the brain was the last mystery of human anatomy, ill described, and with many of its functions only dimly perceived, and its connections to an extensive all-pervading peripheral nervous system, scarcely distinguished. After Willis, the concept of central, peripheral, and autonomic components of a nervous system had been established, and the drawings of the brain and other parts of the nervous system begin to have a modern appearance with only a few errors of omission, simplification or exaggeration.

In this remarkable enrichment of knowledge during Willis's lifetime, in the middle two quarters of the seventeenth century, and in which many participated, his part was the greatest, both in his personal studies, and also in his encouragement of his pupils and colleagues. Evidence of this is not only shown by his numerous anatomical discoveries, but also by the nomenclature that Willis gave to the scientific and medical world. The concept of neurology, and the word itself, which subsequently gave rise to scores of derivatives such as neuroanatomy and neurophysiology, first appears in *Cerebri Anatome*. In the Pordage translation we read: 'we should deliver an exact Neurology or Doctrine of the Nerves', 'we have resolved to undertake the task of the Doctrine of the Nerves', and 'because without the perfect knowledge of the Nerves the Doctrine of the Brain and its Appendix would be left wholly lame and imperfect'. Willis saw anatomy and physiology as a prelude to pathology for we later read 'without these things before known can the Pathology of the Brain and nervous stock be rightly instituted.'

Three characteristics of Willis's work had a most profitable outcome for his research. His singular interest in the nervous system caused his energies and that of his pupils to be directed to this area at a time when many discoveries awaited the scientific explorer. His other productive method of working was to compare studies in human anatomy, comparative anatomy, and experimental studies in animals, with his experience of clinical medicine. In this way, discoveries in anatomy, physiology and clinical medicine went hand in hand in the understanding of the nervous system. Finally, his necropsies were often on his own patients allowing him to relate anatomical changes directly with his clinical experience of that particular case.

In what follows, I have divided the anatomical work of Willis into two parts. The first is the description of the brain and nervous system, as he saw it in 1664, and gave to the world in the writing of *Cerebri Anatome*, and to which he made additions in *De Anima Brutorum* in 1672. Many original anatomical observations appeared in these two books, of which mention will be made. The second part of my commentary is a more detailed analysis of those areas in which Willis gave us an important body of original data. My choice here is of six subjects, the circle of Willis, the cranial nerves, the accessory nerve, the autonomic nervous system, and the spinal cord and its blood supply. Willis's physiological observations were naturally more speculative than his anatomical discoveries, and I have added his theories, where appropriate, after the anatomical structure to which they relate.

Willis's description of the brain and the nervous system is refreshingly readable and parts of his account could be used today in elementary tuition. My own summary is based on a reading of Willis's original Latin, the Pordage translation, the account by Jules Soury,[3] and the interpretation of Hansruedi Isler.[4]

The human brain is parted into two hemispheres, each of which is again divided into an anterior and a posterior lobe by a branch of the carotid artery. The whole surface of the brain consists of gyri and convolutions: thus there is room for a far greater expanse of cortex than under a flat and even surface. The convolutions can be compared to pigeonholes where the impressions of sensible things are stored, and from whence they may be evoked upon suitable occasions. The convolutions are more numerous and of greater size in man than in all other animals because of the various and multiple acts of his superior faculties. In the lesser quadrupeds and in birds and fish, the flat and even surface of the brain is completely devoid of gyri and bends, consequently such animals understand, or learn through imitation, fewer things.

The cerebrum and cerebellum were formerly regarded as mere appendages of the medullary tract but, in Willis's view, they predominate over the medulla which is the common stem of cerebrum and cerebellum. The cerebrum is the primary seat of the rational soul in man, and of the sensitive soul in animals. It is the source of movements and ideas. The activities of the animal come from the cerebrum, whereas the natural functions such as the sensations, movements, passions, instincts, or impulses are controlled to some extent by the cerebrum, but are generated in the cerebellum and in the medulla.

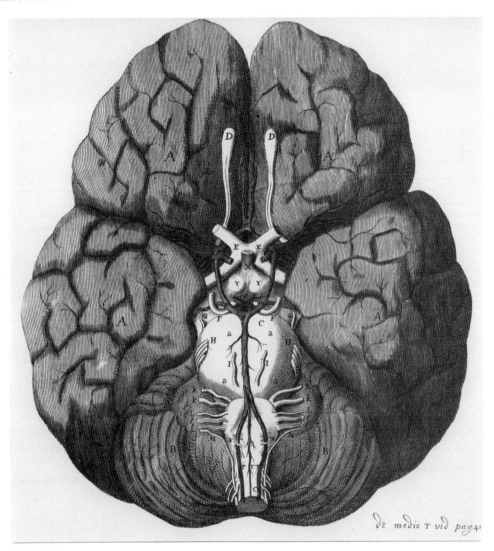

Christopher Wren's drawing of the base of a human brain in Cerebri Anatome.
The Circle of Willis is shown clearly, (Library of Christ Church, Oxford).

The corpus callosum consists of white matter. It receives medullary fibres coming from all the convolutions. It is intended as a market place, where the recently produced spirits gather from every side. Here they stay awhile and begin to perform their functions, either serving imagination or proceeding into the crura of the medulla, causing movements according to requirements in the spinal cord, and in the entrails.

I shall now mention the many anatomical descriptions and illustrations in which Willis broke new ground, a task made easier by the researches of the late Alfred Meyer.[5] The *corpus striatum* and the *optic thalamus* were carefully described by Willis. The notion of basal ganglia was old and Vesalius (1514-

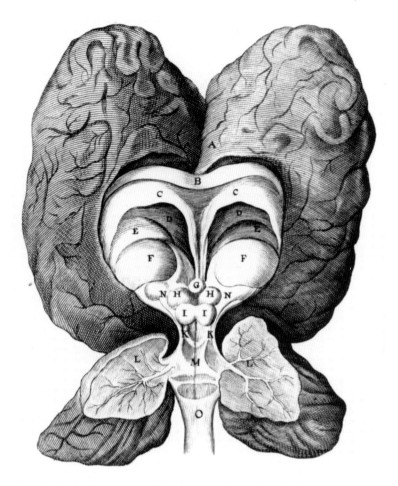

Drawing of a brain from a case of congenital idiocy described in Cerebri Anatome.

1564)[6] had illustrated their anatomical appearance. However, Willis provided a description and also the separate consideration of the striatum from the thalamus. Vesalius did not illustrate the *claustrum* but this appears in Figure 8 of Willis's *De Anima Brutorum* a priority which is sometimes forgotten. The *medullary pyramids* are conspicuous structures but are not especially described before *Cerebri Anatome*, where the name pyramids, given by Willis, first appears. The pyramids were seen and drawn by Bartolommeo Eustachi (1524-1574), an anatomist at Rome, usually called Eustachius. The magnificent drawings of *Tabulae Anatomica* remained in the Papal Library until published in 1714[7] by Giovani Maria Lancisi (1655-1720). It is most unlikely Willis would have been aware of these drawings which antedate his. Willis described and illustrated the *taenia cornua* now called the *stria terminalis*, a tract of fibres connecting the amygdaloid nucleus to several anterior structures. Willis's discovery of the

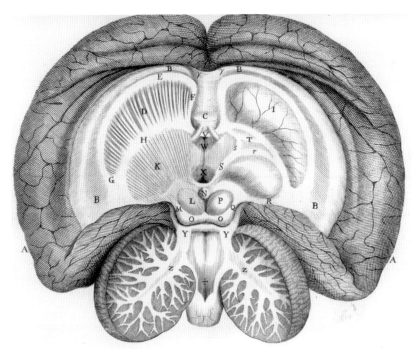

Dissection of the human brain. Drawing from De Anima Brutorum. *The picture shows the structure of the cerebrum and cerebellum, including the central anatomical nuclei and white matter tracts. Some of the anatomical structures depicted appeared here for the first time in print (Library of Christ Church, Oxford).*

anterior commissure should be given recognition. In *Cerebri Anatome* he noted that in the vicinity of the two roots of the fornix 'a transverse medullary tract, resembling a larger nerve, extends from one striate body to the other, and, so to speak, unites these and effects their mutual communication'. This structure, which Willis understood as uniting the corpora striata of the two cerebral hemispheres, was illustrated in Figure 7 of *Cerebri Anatome*. The *internal capsule* is such an important structure in cerebral anatomy and clinical neurology that it is regrettable that Willis's priority in its anatomical description and clinical importance is not more widely known. Vieussens is usually credited with its first description in 1684 but it is clearly illustrated in Figure 8 of *De Anima Brutorum*, and described in the legend. Furthermore in *Cerebri Anatome*, Willis described atrophy of this area in patients with long standing paralysis. This is the first correlation of cortico-spinal tract degeneration with hemiplegia. The discovery of the *inferior olives* by Willis is a further example of the thoroughness of his anatomical studies. They are illustrated and described in *Cerebri Anatome* as *corpora teretia*. The three *cerebellar peduncles* have had several early descriptions by Eustachius and Costanzo Variola (1543-1575) called Variolus but Willis in *Cerebri Anatome* gave the most detailed and accurate description and pictures. Willis first used the word peduncle.

The Circle of Willis

Every doctor in the United Kingdom, and probably those of many other countries, learns as a medical student, of the Circle of Willis, and retains, throughout life, this description of the union and branching of the cerebral arteries at the base of the brain. It is fortunate that the name of Willis is recalled by nomenclature so appropriately bestowed. Many accounts of Willis have focused on his association with the Circle.[8-10] Willis did not claim to have discovered the 'Circle', and he was aware of several previous descriptions and illustrations. Nevertheless, Willis published the first acceptable illustration, made the second good description, correctly surmised its physiological importance, and provided case reports showing the clinical relevance of the circle in medicine. Other predecessors or contemporaries of Willis might have contributed one or more of these observations but none had that overwhelming understanding of the Circle apparent in Willis's writings.

Gabrielle Fallopio (1523-1562) or Fallopius, a pupil of Vesalius, made the first detailed description of these arteries in 1561.[11] The union of the two vertebral arteries into the midline basilar artery is described, and then the division of this artery into right and left branches. The upward course of the carotid arteries and their division into anterior and middle cerebral arteries is described, as is the important early union of the two anterior cerebral arteries. Although the posterior communicating arteries are described, their significance in forming a circle was not appreciated. Guilio Casserio (1561-1616), or Casserius, one of Harvey's teachers in Padua, illustrated an incomplete arterial circle in 1627.[12] Twenty years later Johan Vesling (1598-1649), also in Padua and a correspondent of Harvey, published in a popular anatomy textbook in 1647 a better illustration showing the circle but omitting the all important anastomosis between the two anterior cerebral arteries.[13] Many editions of this work were produced including in 1653, an English translation by Nicholas Culpepper.[14] It is almost certain that Willis would be familiar with the work of Vesling. The next observer was Johan Jakob Wepfer (1620-1695) of Schaffhausen in Switzerland, whose accurate but unillustrated description in 1658 has priority over that of Willis.[15] Wepfer was writing on apoplexy and his patient had a completely occluded right internal carotid artery at the base of the brain, in a patient who died of an abdominal condition, but had experienced left-sided headaches. Wepfer's work is a milestone in our understanding of the pathology of apoplexy and the anatomy of the arterial circle.

The description by Willis of the Circle added little to that of Wepfer but the illustrations provided in *Cerebri Anatome* were superb.

Willis's Figure 1 shows the base of an inverted human brain and Figure 2 a similar view of a sheep's brain. Both these drawings were very likely the work of Christopher Wren. The depiction of the base of a human brain surpassed in

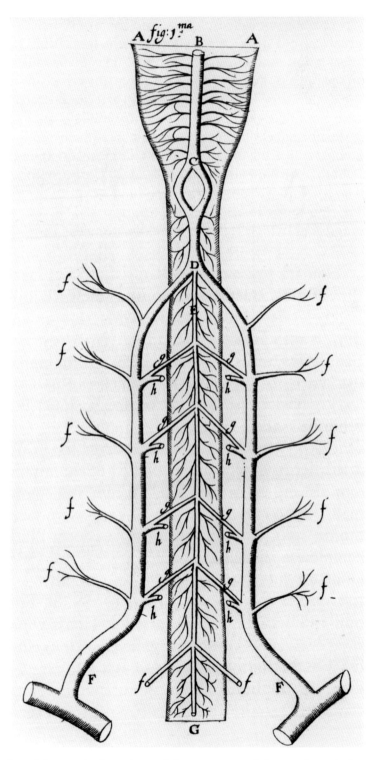

Drawing of the vertebral arteries and the upper part of the anterior spinal artery in
Cerebri Anatome.

accuracy any preceding published picture, and the arterial circle is well seen. The two internal carotid arteries are shown, right larger than left, and they divide into anterior and middle cerebral arteries. This division is acceptable on the left, but on the right is shown as an implausible immediate division into four arteries of comparable size. The anterior cerebral arteries proceed medially and come together in a confluence, a possible but most unlikely anatomical variant. Consequently the normal short anterior communicating artery is not depicted. The posterior communicating arteries are both large, again an unusual variant, for commonly both are small, although in about 20% of cases one is large. The two vertebral arteries are well shown, but the anterior spinal artery is incorrect, and there are no posterior inferior cerebellar arteries. The vertebrals unite to form the basilar artery, which lacks any sizeable branches proceeding laterally

Non ità pridem cujufdam defuncti cadaver diffecuimus, quem *fchirrus* intra mefenterium ingens, ac demum ulcerofus, extinxerat : in eo, dum cranio aperto, quæ ad ἐγκέφαλον pertine-bant luftravimus, *carotidem dextram* intra crani-um emergentem, planè *offeam*, feu potiùs *lapi-deam* (cavitate ejus ferè in totum occlufâ) in-venimus ; adeò ut fanguinis influxu hâc viâ denegato, mirum videatur quare æger non priùs interiiffet Apoplecticus : quod equidem in tan-tum abfuit, ut mentis fuæ, & functionis ani-malis libero exercitio ufque ad extremum vitæ momentum potiretur. Enimvero contra illud Apoplexiæ periculum, natura remedium fatìs idoneum fubftituerat ; nimirum ex eodem la-tere quo *carotis defecerat, Arteria vertebralis*, Tu-buli mole auctâ, *pari fuâ* alterius lateris *triplo major evaferat* : Quippe fanguis *Carotide* exclu-fus, vertebralis folito vectigali fefe infuper ad-dens, & duplicato fluvio in eundem alveum confluens, arteriæ iftius canalem ità fupra modum

Latin text of case report from Willis's medical practice, published in Cerebri Anatome
(Library of Christ Church, Oxford).

over the surface of the pons. The division of the basilar artery into two posterior cerebral arteries is correct but after they receive the posterior communicating arteries, they dwindle in size into arteries smaller than could ever be normal. The impression is of a drawing specially undertaken to show the arterial circle for its physiological importance, but with insufficient care to reproduce faithfully every detail of arterial anatomy.

Willis made several references to the physiological and clinical importance of the circle, of which the case report in *Cerebri Anatome*, pages 95 and 96 is the best example:

Non ita pridem cujusdam defuncti cadaver dissecuimus, quem schirrus intra mesenterium ingens, ac demum ulcerosus, extinxerat: in eo, dum cranio aperto, quae ad pertinebant lustravimus, carotidem dextram intra cranium emergentem, plane osseam, seu potius lapideam (cavitate ejus fere in totum occlusa) invenimus; adeo ut sanguinis influxu hac via denegato, mirum videatur quare aeger non prius interiisset Apoplecticus: quod equidem in tantum abfuit, ut mentis suae, & functionis animalis libero exercitio usque ad extremum vitae momentum potiretur. Enimvero contra ilud Apoplexiae periculum, natura remedium satis idoneum substituerat; nimirum ex eodem latere quo carotis defecerat, Arteria vertebralis, Tubuli mole aucta, part sua alterius lateris triplo major evaserat: Quippe sanguis Carotide exclusus, vertebralis solito vectigali sese insuper addens, & duplicato fluvio in eundem alveum confluens, arteriae istius canalem ita supra modum dilataverat

My translation of this passage is as follows:

It is not long since we dissected the cadaver of a certain man, who died of a large scirhous tumour of the mesentery, which became ulcerated. When his skull was opened we noted amongst the usual intracranial findings, the right carotid artery, in its intracranial part, bony or even stony hard, its lumen being almost totally occluded; so that the influx of blood being denied by this route, it seemed remarkable that this person had not died previously of an apoplexy: which indeed he was so far from, that he enjoyed to the last moments of his life, the free exercise of his mental and bodily functions. For indeed, nature had provided a sufficient remedy against the risk of apoplexy in the vertebral artery of the same side in which the carotid was wanting, since the size of this vessel was enlarged, becoming thrice that of the contralateral vessel: the reason being that because the blood was excluded from the carotid, the required flow added to the perfusion of the vertebral, and flowing in that lumen in twice the amount had enlarged that vessel beyond the normal.

This important account includes the essential clinical record that the patient had normal mental and physical functions before his death from an abdominal tumour. The detailed description of the stenosed carotid artery, and the consequent enlargement of the ipsilateral vertebral artery is part of the evidence that Willis appreciated, not only the anatomy of the arterial circle named after him, but its physiological importance.

The cranial nerves

Of great importance was Willis's description and reclassification of the cranial nerves. Before Willis the classification of Galen (born in Pergamon in 130 AD) had been used for one and a half thousand years. Willis's classification remained in use for some 150 years. Galen recognised seven pairs of cranial nerves, omitting from his classification the olfactory, troclear, and abducens nerves. Willis described the olfactory (1st), optic (2nd), oculomotor (3rd), and troclear (4th) nerves. In describing the trigeminal nerve (5th) he gave the first description of its ophthalmic branch. He described the abducens (6th). His auditory nerve (7th in Willis's classification, but now the 8th) he divided into two branches, and distinguished from the facial nerve. Willis's 8th nerve was the vagus, the subject of an important experiment, described later. The spinal accessory was described for the first time by Willis, who however confused the glossopharygeal nerve with the hypoglossal nerve. This and other minor errors detract from Willis's merit in describing the cranial nerves, but his imperfect classification survived for 150 years.

The accessory nerve

We now come to the anatomical discovery by Willis of the spinal accessory nerve, sometimes called Willis's nerve, the origins, course, and branches of which he studied carefully, as he states:

> Concerning this nerve, because the beginning and distribution of it being very irregular, have not as yet been noted by Anatomists, it may seem worth our labour to make a little more diligent inquiry.

Willis was indeed curious about this nerve of his own discovery.

The autonomic nervous system

The modern literature of the autonomic nervous system can be said to begin with Willis's *Cerebri Anatome*.[16] Willis was interested in what he termed the Wandering Nerve (our vagus nerve), and numbered by him the '8th nerve', and the sympathetic trunk. He was so diligent in tracing the branches of these nerves to the viscera that he clearly was impressed by the innervation of the heart, lungs and abdominal organs. Willis describes how the nerves from the vagus and sympathetic trunk wound around the arteries and veins, which were invested by 'thickset rows of processes'. He had an excellent understanding of the function of this innervation of the vessels, which was to deliver a constant supply of spirits so that they might 'imitate the movement of the heart'. The blood vessels were 'constricted by this kind of nervous bridles [which] moderate the course of the blood according to the impulses of the passions'. Willis would have easily understood the workings of a modern lie-detector. A very important detail was the description of a branch of the vagus nerve going to the arch of the aorta. Sheehan has described this as the earliest reference to the depressor nerve. Willis's experiment of the bilateral ligation of the vagus nerve in a dog was a model of a scientific question answered by an experiment. He wished to know whether the pulse of the heart depended on the supply of spirits from the vagus nerves. The dog developed cardiac irregularities and convulsions, probably due to cerebral ischaemia. Finally Willis, and Richard Lower, gave us a fine drawing of the autonomic nervous system in *Cerebri Anatome*, the first good diagram of this component of the nervous system. Its great merit was to draw separately the vagus nerve from the sympathetic trunk. Willis erred in representing a communication between the sympathetic trunk and the brain apparently through the trigeminal nerve and his VI nerve (the abducent).

The spinal cord and its blood supply

The first accurate description of the blood supply of the spinal cord appears in *Cerebri Anatome*, and a detailed account of this part of Willis's work appears elsewhere.[17] Willis's descriptions of the brain are better known than his observations on the spinal cord, which nevertheless were of considerable importance. He described and illustrated the cervical and lumbo-sacral enlargements, and the anterior and posterior nerve roots. He seemed not to have appreciated the different function of the anterior and posterior nerve roots, which I regret, since he put forward the first description of reflex action. Willis's concept of reflex action was clearer than that of Descartes, although he was in error in his belief that the impulse journeyed to and from the brain. These theories of the passage of nerve impulses are the more remarkable since they antedate the discovery of electric current.

The first modern description and illustration of the blood supply of the spinal cord is that in *Cerebri Anatome*. Willis took advantage of fetal specimens and made some injection studies. Richard Lower probably helped in the dissections and may have drawn the illustrations. Willis showed clearly the union of the two anterior spinal branches from the vertebral arteries to form the anterior spinal artery, which is shown receiving tributaries accompanying the nerve roots. The posterior spinal arteries and the spinal veins are also described and illustrated.

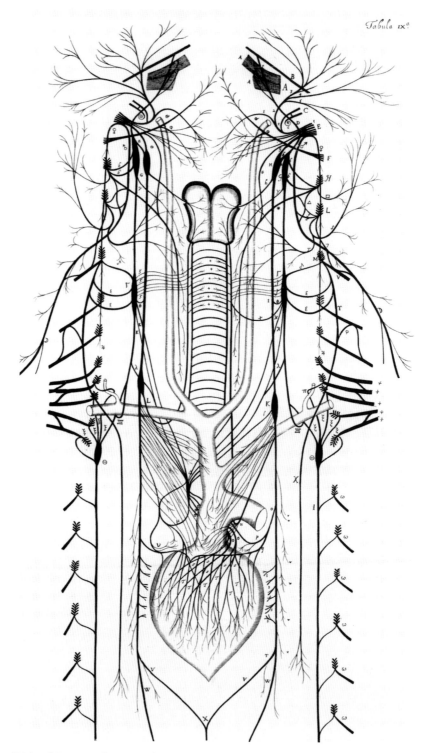

Richard Lower's drawing of the autonomic nervous system in Cerebri Anatome.
Note the accessory nerve and the innervation of the heart.

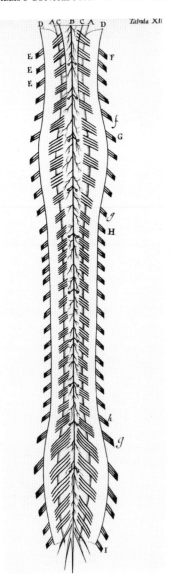

The human spinal cord and its blood supply viewed from its anterior aspect in Cerebri Anatome.

This description and illustration was not bettered until those of Albrech von Haller.

Willis is remembered for his 'Circle', and the justice of this eponym has been argued. There are four other anatomical usages and one physical sign, which require comment. *Chordae Willisii* are the endothelial clad trabeculae which pass across the meningeal blood sinuses. The *'nervus ophthalmicus Willisii'* is the first division of the trigeminal nerve, and the *'nervus accessorium Willisii'* is the spinal accessory nerve. So many practitioners have cause to be grateful to Willis, whose reputation will be ever green with otologists from the symptom of *'paracusis Willisii'*, a valuable clue to the integrity of the auditory nerve in a case of deafness.

REFERENCES

1   Heinrich Boruttau. In: *Handbuch der Geschichte der Medicin*, Vol 2, edited by T. Puschmann. Jena: 1903, p 327.

2   R Brain. The concept of hysteria in the time of William Harvey. *Proceedings of the Royal Society of Medicine*, 1963, Vol 56, pp 321-3.

3   Jules Soury. *Le Systeme Nerveux Central*, Vol. 1. Paris: 1898.

4   Hansruedi Isler. *Thomas Willis, 1621-1675: Doctor and Scientist*. New York: Hafner, 1968.

5   A Meyer. *Historical Aspects of Cerebral Anatomy*. London, New York, Toronto: Oxford University Press, 1971.

6   Andreas Vesalius. *De Humani Corporis Fabrica*. Basileae, 1543.

7   Bartolommeo Eustachi. *Tabulae Anatomicae*, edited by JM Lancisi. Rome, 1714.

8   Sir Charles Symonds. Harveian Oration. The Circle of Willis. *British Medical Journal*, Vol 1, 1955, 119-24.

9   Alfred Meyer and Raymond Hierons, Observations on the history of the 'Circle of Willis', *Medical History*, 1962, Vol 6, pp 119-30.

10   E Steven Gurdjian and Edwin S Gurdjian, History of Occlusive Cerebrovascular Disease, 1. From Wepfer to Moniz. *Archives of Neurology*, 1979, Vol 36, 341-3.

11   G Fallopius. *Observationes Anatomicae*. Venice: 1561.

12   J Casserius. 78 Tabulae anatomicae. In: Adrianni Spigeli's *De Humani Corporis Fabrica Libri Decem*. Venice: 1627.

13   J Vesling. *Syntagma Anatomicum*. Padua: 1647.

14   J Vesling. *The Anatomy of the Body of Man*. Translated by N Culpepper. London: 1653.

15   JJ Wepfer. *Observationes Anatomicae ex Cadaveribus Eorum Quos Sustulit Apoplexia (cum Exercitatione de Eious Loco Affecto)*. Schaffusi: JC Suteri, 1658.

16   D Sheehan. Discovery of the autonomic nervous system. *Archives of Neurology and Psychiatry*, 1936, vol 36, 1081-115.

17   J Trevor Hughes. Spinal cord arteries described by Willis. Chap 20. In: *Historical Aspects of the Neurosciences*, edited by F Clifford Rose and WF Bynum. New York: Raven Press, 1982.

Chapter 9

Willis's Concepts of Life Processes, and of Diseases and their Treatment

'So I say, both of Galen and Paracelsus'
(All's Well that Ends Well, Act 11, Scene 3)
William Shakespeare

To the enquiry of Lafeu, if the King's illness is incurable, Parolles replies yes, whether treated by the measures of Galen or of Paracelsus. In Shakespeare's time there was an even handed choice between the old and the new remedies. In Willis's day successful medical practice entailed a constant search for new remedies for diseases, since, to an astute physician, it was clear that, with very few exceptions, most diseases were unaffected by any of the traditional remedies. Willis, despite being at first surrounded by the formal teaching of Hippocrates and Galen in the medical curriculum of the University, was always a Paracelsian.

The ideas of Paracelsus in medical treatment were thought revolutionary by his contemporary sixteenth century doctors, and considerable time elapsed before this profound challenge to the teachings of Galen gained any general acceptance. Helmont was greatly influenced by Paracelsus, and Willis in turn read Helmont and other interpreters of Paracelsus. Those medical practitioners and apothecaries, who accepted new ideas of diseases and sought new remedies, were called Paracelsists, Helmontians, Spagyrists, Chemiastrists, or Iatrochemists. Willis was a leader in England of this new concept of disease and its treatment. He had many followers, who were themselves a minor school of iatrochemists, and would sometimes be referred to as Willisians. Willis seemed, from the onset of his medical career, to be receptive to new ideas of the causes of diseases and to novel therapeutic measures. He clearly had an unusually enquiring mind but also, due to the special circumstances in Oxford, he largely missed the stifling effect of a traditional medical education. He was also in contact with many innovative doctors and scientists, as described in Chapters 4 and 6.

Willis wrote well, and was so constantly productive up to his death, that we may study his views of diseases and their treatment serially in his published works. The analyses of these by Hansruedi Isler is recommended,[1] as is that of Robert G Frank Jr.[2] We have seven to consider, and are also fortunate in having the casebook of Willis and John Locke's notebook of Willis's lectures, both edited and published by the late Kenneth Dewhurst.[3,4] These sources allow us an excellent insight into Willis's theories which extended far beyond medicine. Theories of air were explored to explain respiration, combustion, and explosions. Fermentation and putrefaction were studied to explain normal vital processes in the whole living world and their derangement in illness and death. Speculation on the causation of diseases traditionally was directed to an all-embracing theory of disease. Despite the scientific advances at this time of the seventeenth century, no disease was understood in a modern way. The scientific basis underlying infectious diseases, nutritional diseases, genetic diseases, degenerative diseases, and toxic diseases (except poisoning) was not known. Even that a rational basis for each disease might exist was not universally realised, nor were individual diseases separated beyond their symptoms. In appraising Willis we must bear in mind the current state of knowledge in the mid-seventeenth century, and not judge him by the standards of the twentieth century, which, in any case, will be eclipsed by the standards of the twenty-first century. Willis's speculations and theories concern so many areas that this review will be confined to the headings given.

Life

Living creatures are divided into four classes. The first, and lowest, consists of plants, worms, and other creatures whose parts are homogeneous, and whose life is slow. The second class of life are creatures such as insects, who although bloodless, yet have a circulating fluid, which conveys their vital processes. The third class are animals, which possess a blood circulation, but not having a second ventricle to the heart, do not use pulmonary ventilation, as developed by the fourth and highest class. The fourth class are warm blooded animals with twin ventricles allowing a circulation through the lungs by which some nitrous element is taken from the air.

Respiration

Life and respiration are comparable to a burning lamp, which requires three components, the vessel, oil to burn, and air without which the lamp is extinguished. In a living man the heart is the vessel, the blood is the oil, and air drawn into the lungs is the third component, all being essential for life. This analogy led Willis into an explanation of several diseases. The heart (lamp) may not function, there may be a loss of blood (oil) from haemorrhage, and obstruction of the intake of air in suffocation caused death. This account now seems naive but in Willis's day even the circulation of the blood was a recent concept. Willis believed bodily activities were coordinated by a 'corporeal soul' of two parts, the 'vital soul' which was a 'flame' in the blood and the 'sensitive soul' which were the animal spirits diffused throughout the brain and nervous system.

The 'flame' in the blood was fed by sulphurous matter from the food and nitrous particles from the air. Willis in his later works showed how earthworms breathed and how fish and the oyster had gills allowing them to take in nitrous particles from the water.

Fermentation

In June 1656 Willis had completed 'De fermentione', which was published in 1659 in *Diatribae Duae Medico-philosophicae*. Willis was very intrigued by fermentation, which he had observed in the making of bread with yeast, in the production of beer, wine, and vinegar, and in the curdling of milk to make cheese. He described the process as 'whatsoever Effervency or Turgency, that is raised up in a Natural Body, by particles of that body variously agitated'. Many substances were subject to fermentation but only if they contain heterogenous particles. The simpler products of the 'Chymists' were stable, whilst compound liquors, such as the juices of plants, or the blood of animals, begin to ferment after a short while. A herbal distillate may remain unchanged, but if mixed with sugar, will become sour and spoil. These observations still have validity but Willis's attempts to explain many life processes and several diseases as forms of fermentation led him astray.

The five chemical principles

Willis was critical of the Aristotelian doctrine of four elements, Water, Fire, Air, and Earth, and himself proposed to accept the 'doctrine of the Chymists' that all bodies could be analysed into particles of spirit, sulphur, salt, water, and earth. Willis thought that an excess of one, or a deficiency of another, or an unstable mixture of two or more was the explanation of certain diseases. At first sight this seems as ludicrous as Aristotle, but it contains the realisation that some recognisable chemical compounds are included in the makeup of living things. Besides, dehydration and salt depletion remain medical conditions, which are treated by remedying the specific deficiency. Little further progress could be made in Willis's day when no elements had been recognised as such, and no chemical compound had been separated into its component elements.

Sensation and pain

Sensation occurs when an external sensory object affects, by its movement or shape, the spirits lodged in its nervous parts, which are excited to a similar movement. Pain is an annoying sensation as pleasure is an agreeable one. Pain results from external and internal causes. External causes are disproportionate objects hitting the body from without, or taken internally, such as medicines or other unpleasant things (it seems medicine was always unpleasant). Internal causes include flatulence, which is generated in the stomach and intestines as when acid of vitriol is poured on dust of coral. Colic is not caused by the flatulence of distension but by a convulsion of parts of the intestines.

Movement and muscular contraction

As sensation is the communication inwards of external motion, so movement, initiated by the cerebrum, passes outwards, using spirits communicated along the nerves. These spirits excited the spirits lodging in the muscles into expansion. The account of muscular contraction above comes from John Locke's Notebook, and is an acceptable theory of muscle contraction. Willis however was intrigued with chemical explosions, and himself experimented with *aurum fulminans*. This work on the explosions of inorganic chemicals prompted him to theorise that the contraction of muscle was a form of explosion, inflating and contracting the belly of the muscle. This theory appears in *Cerebri Anatome*, where he suggests that spirits in muscle fibres, including spirituous-saline particles, ignite and explode in the way that the combination of nitre and sulphur explodes. This theory, called *explosio Willisiana*, was much criticised and today seems absurd. We now know the ultrastructure of muscular contraction as seen by the electron microscope in the mid-twentieth century, but details of its chemistry are still obscure.

Wakefulness, sleep, and the action of narcotics

Willis theorised a great deal on these subjects still imperfectly understood towards the close of the twentieth century. He made many pertinent observations. Control from the medulla oblongata is described, and the essential continuance of the function of the heart, lungs and intestines is given as evidence that some action of the brain must continue in sleep, though Willis localises this to the cerebellum. Willis theorises on insomnia, sleepwalking, and narcosis, and in describing the loss of recent memory in a patient who had taken a narcotic, comes near to an understanding of the positive aspect of sleep in memory function. Willis extends his observations into lethargy and coma, with the conviction, not then generally accepted, that all these states are due to action or inaction of the brain.

Lethargy and coma

Willis was interested in what he termed lethargy, and clearly thought deeply of his many cases with a lowering of consciousness. He studied some cases in 1661 of an epidemic fever in Oxford which he described as a 'new' disease. This was quite probably an epidemic of encephalitis lethargica, and has been described in detail by Donald G Bates.[5] Other cases with fever may have been cases of meningitis. One of his lethargic cases had obstructive hydrocephalus from meningitis, as shown by a necropsy when his brain 'abounded with a watery humour'. Another case with lethargy and severe headaches died of an intracranial tumour, probably a meningioma.[6] Other cases were due to cerebral ischaemia caused by cerebro-vascular disease. He recognised the lethargy of congenital imbecility and also that of the cerebral degeneration of old age.

Delirium, phrenzy, and mania

Delirium is a turmoil of the spirits of the cerebrum. It arises in fevers from the blood carrying to the brain wild and untamed components which agitate the spirits. Delirium can also occur from wounds, gangrenous conditions, and excesses of drugs. Phrenzy is caused by the carriage to the brain of hostile matter from serious fevers such as smallpox and the plague. Necropsies show that meningitis and purulent states of the brain do not cause phrenzy, but lethargy and coma. Mania is a delirium without fever but with fury and boldness. Willis describes mania in detail and clearly understands it as a disturbance of affect, and is obviously aware of manic-depressive psychosis. He also knows the mania of rabies even to the detail that either the bite or the saliva of the rabid animal will cause the disease.

Melancholia and hysteria

Willis defines melancholia as delirium with fear and sadness but without fever. The melancholia could be general, affecting all matters, or particular, when the phantasy goes astray only on one matter, but imagination and reason are correct on all others. The condition may begin from fear, worry, sadness, love, or intense study. Willis was familiar with what he termed habitual melancholy, and also recognised occasional melancholy. Clearly Willis observed with great understanding the various psychiatric disturbances in his patients. The hypotheses he framed to explain these psychiatric conditions were fanciful but even today, in some of these disorders, no better explanation has been suggested. Willis's views on hysteria attracted great attention during his lifetime. Willis was convinced that hysteria was a condition caused by dysfunction of the brain. He dismissed any idea that the symptoms arose from the uterus, the spleen, or the lungs. The condition was common in widows and virgins, and occurred in men, so an explanation that hysteria was caused by the upward movement of the womb to the diaphragm was dismissed by Willis. He did not believe, as did Sydenham, that congestion of the lungs caused hysteria, since he did not see hysteria in pneumonia and other pulmonary states. Willis and his champions successfully resisted all arguments against his views on hysteria.

Willis's pharmacology

The pharmacopoeia of Willis is known in some detail from his publication of *Pharmaceutice Rationalis*, towards the end of his life. It appeared in two parts, published in Oxford, the first in 1674, and the second a few days after his death in November 1675. It begins with a laudable plea for a rational scientific basis for pharmacology, not however realisable in that century. Willis complained that pharmacology had been studied empirically rather than scientifically. So far, knowledge was confined to the compounding of drugs, and the determination of their dosages and the diseases for which they were appropriate. Explanations as to where in the body they had their effect and how they acted were totally lacking. As with other branches of science, pharmacology had to be based on relevant experiments and critical observation on the effects on patients. Only in this way could ineffective and dangerous treatments be avoided. Rational pharmacology would absolve qualified doctors from their critics, who were often correct in denouncing harsh and ineffective treatments. Here Willis speaks as a twentieth century pharmacologist rather than one 300 years earlier, and we must give him credit for his intentions and forgive his inability to carry them out. The *Pharmaceutice* was a brave attempt at rational pharmacology. Willis describes vomiting, detailing the anatomy of the stomach, oesophagus, and intestines, and also the innervation of these structures and how some emetics act on the medulla oblongata. He discusses constipation and diarrhoea and their treatment with laxatives and drugs against the dysenteric diseases. He distinguishes purges which act by the irritation of the intestines from others, which pass into the blood, noting that the aroma of cathartic medicines may often be detected in the sweat and urine. Diaphoretics are described with explanations of the mechanisms of sweating. The mechanism of urine production is discussed and observations included on excessive diuresis. Part 1 contains the famous distinction between the urine of diabetes and of renal failure. Drugs affecting the heart are described. Willis's observations on sedatives and hypnotics are numerous. He had studied the effect of opiates, not only on his patients but experimentally on dogs who could take large amounts, and on cats, who in company with most animals would succumb to a large dose. The rapid effect of opiates intravenously in dogs was studied.

The second part of *Pharmaceutice Rationalis* disappoints, as despite Willis's earlier brave words, he resorts to remedies such as blood-letting, purgation, blistering, branding, and the induction of vomiting. The work abounds however with accurate and sometimes original clinical descriptions. This is Willis's last work, finished in the closing weeks of his life, and its perusal evokes a feeling of poignancy for the author in 1675. Willis is well aware of the need for rational pharmacology; throughout his medical career, he has striven to prepare and use remedies from the new 'chymistry'; but, at the end of his life, the orderly scientific use of drugs completely eludes him, as it did for medical practitioners in the succeeding centuries.

REFERENCES

1   H Isler. *Thomas Willis, 1621-1675: Doctor and Scientist*. New York and London: Hafner, 1968.

2   RG Frank Jr. *Harvey and the Oxford Physiologists*. Berkeley, Los Angeles and London: University of California Press, 1980.

3   K Dewhurst. *Thomas Willis's Oxford Lectures*. Oxford: Sandford Publications, 1980.

4   K Dewhurst. *Willis's Casebook*. Oxford: Sandford Publications, 1981.

5   DG Bates. Thomas Willis and the Epidemic Fever of 1661: a commentary. *Bulletin of the History of Medicine*, 1965, Vol 39, pp 393-414.

6   JT Hughes. Thomas Willis, the First Oxford neuropathologist. In: *Neurology Across the Centuries*, edited by FC Rose. London: Smith-Gordon: Niigata, Nishimura: 1989, pp 87-96.

Chapter 10
Diseases and Syndromes
Recognised by Willis

His observations on the natural history of diseases were
accurate and many of them original
Sir Charles Symonds[1]

Remarkable in the achievements of Willis were the numerous diseases and distinctive groups of symptoms that he recognised during his medical practice.[2] These original observations are so numerous that some order is required in their listing and analysis. What follows is first a consideration of four diseases or syndromes whose first recognition by Willis is scarcely disputed. These are *achalasia of the cardia, akathisia, myasthenia gravis*, and *paracusis Willisii*. The medical literature of these four conditions virtually begins with the writing of Willis. In each case I give my own modern translation instead of or as well as that of Pordage. Naturally, these conditions are rarer than those in a longer list of diseases either recognised imperfectly by Willis or whose description followed that of others. Willis's contribution to the study of these diseases is of historical importance. The list includes such common conditions as asthma, diabetes, dementia, encephalitis lethargica, epilepsy, narcolepsy, neurosyphilis, puerperal fever, pulmonary diseases, tuberculosis, typhoid fever, and typhus fever.

Achalasia of the cardia

The old name of cardiospasm has now been replaced by achalasia of the oesophagus or achalasia of the cardiac orifice of the stomach. The modern concept of this disease is that of a chronic disorder of muscle motility causing obstruction at the sphincter between the oesophagus and the stomach. The clinical syndrome arises from the failure to relax (achalasia) of this sphincter during swallowing. This failure to relax can be observed radiologically, and the physiology of deglutition can be shown to be imperfect. Anatomically, depletion of the ganglion cells of Auerbach's plexus, serving this sphincter, can be demonstrated in some but not all cases.

Willis not only recognised this syndrome but devised the means of its treatment. The most relevant passage occurs in Part 1 of *Pharmaceutice Rationalis*, 1674, which I translate as:

A rare case of an Oxford man demonstrates how continuous vomiting may be caused by occlusion of the cardiac orifice of the stomach. A strong man, otherwise healthy, suffered from repeated vomiting, usually casting up whatsoever he had eaten . . . Medicines were of no avail, he languished from hunger and was in danger of death. From whalebone, I made for him a rod with a button of sponge fixed to the tip. My patient, having eaten his meat and drink, would then thrust my instrument down his oesophagus, through the cardia into the stomach. The cardia being opened, the food, which otherwise would have returned, passed into the stomach. By this means he has daily taken his sustenance for fifteen years, and is yet alive and well, when otherwise he would have perished from hunger.

Akathisia

Akathisia, or the restless legs syndrome, is best known as a familial disorder inherited as an autosomal dominant, and then frequently known as Ekbom's syndrome.[3] It is a generalised sensory disturbance affecting arms as well as legs, so that all limbs are subjected to a compulsive urge to movement. The subject experiences distressing tension accompanying a need to move and walk about. The syndrome is also seen as a complication of the treatment of Parkinson's disease with dopaminergic drugs. There is strong evidence that the cause of the inherited syndrome is a disorder of dopamine metabolism, manifest as an overproduction of dopamine, and the cause of the iatrogenic disease in the treatment of Parkinson's disease is excessive administration of dopamine drugs. The first recognisable report of akathisia is by Willis which the Pordage translation gives as:

> These patients retire to bed, but presently, in their arms and legs, arise movements of the whole limbs and twitchings of the muscles. So great is the muscle restlessness, that the distressed patients are no more able to sleep than if they were in a place of torture.

Myasthenia gravis[4]

We now come to the disease myasthenia gravis, in which the voluntary muscles tire with activity, but recover with rest. Not only are the muscles of the limbs and trunk affected but also those innervated by the cranial nerves, with consequent transient paresis of the eye muscles, and those subserving facial movements and swallowing. The syndrome is caused by a disorder of acetyl choline metabolism, probably through an auto-immune response forming an antibody to muscle end-plate protein. From this it follows that thymectomy permanently benefits the disease, and the paresis can be temporarily improved by the administration of prostigmin, which acts as an anti-cholinesterase, and allows the accumulation of acetyl choline at the motor end plate.

The first clear description of myasthenia gravis was by Willis, and is found in *De Anima Brutorum*, where there are several descriptions of the condition, with which Willis was clearly familiar. The passages occur towards the middle of the section entitled 'Of the Palsy'. Willis makes a distinction between 'habitual palsy' and 'spurious palsy' and makes the observation that there are patients who lie in bed from excessive weakness, yet have normal gastro-intestinal function, a healthy pulse, and normal urine. The curiosity of their muscle weakness is that in the morning they are able to walk normally, use their limbs, and lift heavy objects. Yet, before noon their energy is spent and they cannot move hand or foot. This is a clear description of generalised myasthenia with fatiguability recovering with rest. Willis also noted the same phenomenon affecting the muscles innervated by the cranial nerves, in a very significant case which I translate concisely as:

> I have a patient, a prudent and honest woman, who for many years has been subject to this type of spurious palsy, not only affecting her limbs, but also her tongue. She speaks freely, and readily enough, for a while, but after a long period of speech, or if she speaks hastily or eagerly, she is not able to speak a word, and is as mute as a fish. Her voice does not return for one or two hours.

In the section of *De Anima Brutorum* titled 'On seeing' a case report of a young man with diplopia was thought by Sir Geoffrey Keynes to be another case of myasthenia gravis.

It is a feature of the writings of Willis that he frequently speculates about the cause of a disease. Sometimes this leads him to a theory of the disease which, by modern standards, is absurd, but in the case of myasthenia gravis, his thoughts have a strangely modern ring. The relevant passage in the Pordage translation is:

> In this kind of spurious palsie ... it may be suspected, that not only the Spirits themselves are at fault, but besides, that sometimes the imbecility and impotence of local motion doth in some measure also depend upon the fault of the explosive Copula suffused everywhere from the blood to the moving parts.

Pordage had very little understanding of the work he was translating and my modern concise translation might be as follows:

> In this type of transient paresis, arising from the absence, or marked reduction, of some required hormone, the paretic effect may be due to a hormonal deficiency in which the required agent is unable to move from the blood into the muscle fibres.

The quotations above demonstrate that Willis, not only recognised the syndrome but had theories of its causation, which are still relevant. For the next recognisable description of a myasthenic patient, the medical world had to await the paper by Sir Samuel Wilks in 1877, a more complete account by Erb in 1879, and a definitive account by Goldflam in 1893. The disease has been known as Erb-Goldflam disease, a name now in disuse, fortunately, since it ignores the prior claim of Willis. It is of interest that the famous medical textbook. *Principles and Practice of Medicine*, published in 1892 by Sir William Osler, who was inclined to disparage Willis, did not include an account of myasthenia gravis.

Paracusis Willisii

There is a phenomenon, well known to specialists of ear diseases, and which is experienced by certain deaf patients, whose hearing improves in the presence of noise. The deafness may be so profound as to prevent normal conversation, but in the noise, for example of a railway train, a conversation can be heard by the otherwise deaf passenger. This symptom excludes nerve deafness and indicates an obstruction in conduction. It is most likely to be due to stapes fixation and the commonest cause is otosclerosis.

Paracusis is well described in *De Anima Brutorum* in the section 'On hearing':

> For we meet with a certain kind of deafness, in which those affected, seem wholly to want the Sense of Hearing, yet as soon as a great noise, as of great Guns, Bells, or Drums, is made near to the Ears, they distinctly hear the speeches of the by-standers, but this great noise ceasing, they presently grow deaf again.

The following passage includes two cases reports, the first being:

> a Woman, tho she were deaf, yet so long as a Drum was beaten within her Chamber, she heard every word perfectly; wherefore her Husband kept a Drummer on purpose for his servant, that by that means he might have some converse with his Wife.

and the second:

> another Deaf Person, who living near a Ring of Bells, as often as they all rung out, he could easily hear any word, and not else.

There follows brief notes and references to the numerous common diseases in the literature of which Willis is quoted.

Asthma and emphysema[5]

Willis probably gave the first acceptable modern descriptions of asthma and emphysema.[6] His long and detailed description of asthma includes a clear understanding of bronchospasm, for which, in his opinion, there might be a nervous cause. The first clinical and pathological account of emphysema appears in Part 1 of *Pharmaceutice Rationalis*.

Diabetes mellitis[7]

The jewel of discovery in *Pharmaceutice Rationalis* is the description of diabetes mellitus, the 'pissing evil'. Willis recognised the sweetness of the urine and the distinction from the polyuria of renal disease. His account is important in the history of knowledge of the disease in Europe, although other observations in the East outdate Willis. However, Willis also described what was probably diabetic neuritis:

> ... I have observed in many people who have been subject to his disease . . .
> they felt flying, running pains through their whole Bodies, and corrugations
> sometimes with dizziness or stinging ...

Dementia[8]

Willis's views on dementia have been described in Chapter 9. He wrote extensively and enigmatically on a favourite subject, and his writings are discussed in the work cited above.

Encephalitis lethargica[9]

Willis was such an acute observer and such a rigorous scientist that his 'Description of an Epidemical Fever chiefly infectious to the Brain and Nervous Stock, spreading in the year 1661' in *Pathologiae Cerebri* is perplexing and full of interest. Willis was describing an epidemic of a fever new to him, and the account by Bates, cited above, argues that the condition was probably an epidemic of encephalitis lethargica.

Epilepsy[10]

The history of epilepsy 'The Sacred Disease' has such a voluminous literature, that a perusal of the analytical work of Owsei Tempkin is profitable. Tempkin gave many pages in his work to a consideration of Willis's observations and theories of epilepsy. He accepted the division into idiopathic and sympathetic and was aware, as were the ancients, of the effect of irritation of the brain. He was sure that epilepsy arose in the brain and knew cases of epilepsy caused by external stimuli, explained by his (original) theories of reflex action. He disagreed that the meninges or the cerebral ventricles were the source of the convulsions.

Epidemic fevers[11]

Willis studied many types of fevers, and his report of three epidemics in 1657 and 1658 was, according to Sir George Creighton, cited above, the first systematic piece of epidemiology written in England. In 1643 Willis observed the famous 'camp fever' of the Civil War, which was very likely typhus. He distinguished it later from cases of typhoid fever. Willis described the recurrent paroxysms of fever of malaria, and saw several epidemics of smallpox and plague.

Neurosyphilis[6]

Willis is often credited with the first description of General Paralysis of the Insane, a disease which he must frequently have encountered. In the opinion of Hierons, the cases referred to may have had other pathology such as cerebro-vascular disease. However other case reports, in *Pharmaceutice Rationalis*, are reminiscent of tabes dorsalis.

Narcolepsy[12]

In *De Anima Brutorum* Willis describes in great detail the normal process of sleep, discussed in Chapter 9, and the disorders of sleep. His cases of excessive somnolence would now be diagnosed as narcolepsy.

Puerperal fever[13]

De Febribus the second part of *Diatribae* (1659), contains an excellent account of puerperal fever, with the first modern terminology of the condition.

Tuberculosis and pulmonary diseases[14]

Willis studied the macroscopical and microscopical structure of the normal lung, providing the best anatomical description then available, and including the discovery of the lymphatics. He made numerous autopsies on pulmonary diseases noting, amongst other observations, the changes of chronic pulmonary tuberculosis with calcification of the hilar lymph nodes. He was well aware of the differences between this chronic fibroid type and the more fatal acute disseminated form, and the spread of the disease to the neck, intestinal tract and to the bones. Naturally, a disease as prevalent as tuberculosis has a literature extending for centuries, but the description of Willis is still noteworthy.

The account above omits several common diseases known to Willis as well as many perplexing cases still awaiting analysis, but does substantiate my belief that the reputation of Thomas Willis will continue to grow because of the diseases and syndromes recognised by him. The encyclopedic work of Dr Major on 'Classic Descriptions of Disease' is a good measure of the fame of our past doctors.[2] Dr Major included six entries from the works of Willis, more than from the writings of any other person.

REFERENCES

1   C Symonds. Thomas Willis, FRS (1621-1675). In: *The Royal Society, Its Origins and Founders*, edited by Sir Harold Hartley, London: 1960.

2   RH Major. *Classic Descriptions of Diseases*, 3rd edn. Oxford: Blackwell Scientific Publications, 1955.

3   K Ekbom. Restless legs syndrome, *Neurology*, 1960, Vol 10, pp 868-73.

4   G Keynes. The history of myasthenia gravis, *Medical History*, 1961, Vol 5, pp 313-26.

5   RH Major, *op. cit.* pp 577-80.

6   R Hierons. Willis's Contributions to clinical medicine and neurology. *Journal of the Neurological Sciences*, 1967, Vol 4, pp 1-13.

7   FN Allan. The writings of Thomas Willis, MD: diabetes three hundred years ago, *Diabetes*, 1953, Vol 2, pp 74-8.

8   B Clarke. *Mental Disorder in Earlier Britain*. Cardiff: University of Wales Press, 1975.

9   DB Bates. Thomas Willis and the epidemic fever of 1661, *Bulletin of the History of Medicine*, 1965, Vol 39, pp 393-414.

10   O Temkin. *The Falling Sickness*, 2nd edn. Baltimore and London: Johns Hopkins University Press, 1971.

11   C Creighton. *A History of Epidemics in Britain*, 2 Vols. Cambridge: Cambridge University Press, 1891-1894. Reprinted by London: Frank Cass, 1965.

12   WC Lennox. Thomas Willis on Narcolepsy, *Archives of Neurology and Psychiatry*, 1939, Vol 41, pp 348-51.

13   CH Peckham. A brief history of puerperal infection. *Bulletin of the Institute of The History of Medicine*, 1935, Vol 3, p 192.

14   DS Miller. Thomas Willis and his *De Phthisi Pulmonari*. *American Review of Tuberculosis*, 1922, Vol 5, pp 934-49.

Chapter 11

Willis in London

he became so noted, and so infinitely resorted to, for his practice,
that never any physician before went beyond him, or got more
Money yearly than he

Anthony Wood (1632-1695)

In the autumn of 1667, Willis moved his place of work and his residence to the City of Westminster, now part of Greater London, but then more distinct from the City of London. In moving to London he was greatly encouraged by the support of his old friend and patron Gilbert Sheldon, who also wanted Willis in London because of the illnesses in that city and a personal medical problem. Sheldon, when Warden of All Souls, Oxford, had appointed Willis to the chair of Natural Philosophy, but since 1663, as the Archbishop of Canterbury, had lived in Lambeth Palace on the Thames directly opposite Westminster. Sheldon had a high regard for Willis as a person and as a doctor, but was also greatly concerned by the distress in London of the terrible outbreak of Plague in 1665. The doctors in London had been impotent in the face of this great medical and social calamity, and the status of the medical profession, and particularly of the Royal College of Physicians had suffered. It is possible that Willis journeyed to Lambeth to give advice and it is likely that his pamphlet 'A plain and Easie Method for Preserving (by God's Blessing) those who are well from Infection of the Plague . . .' was prepared in haste in order to be sent to Sheldon. The Archbishop in London was overwhelmed by the pastoral cares of the plague stricken city when he himself suffered a medical calamity in the form of a cerebral stroke. It is almost certain that Willis was consulted for, in *De Anima Brutorum*, there is an exact description of this illness:

> The most Reverend Father in God the Lord Gilbert Archbishop of Canterbury, recovered of a grievous Apoplectical Fit, six years ago, (God prospering our medicinal help, to whom we render eternal thanks) from that time, though he sometimes suffer'd some light skirmishes of the Disease, yet he never fell, or became speechless or senseless.

It can be surmised that the encouragement of Sheldon was most persuasive in Willis's decision to move, and a summons by the Archbishop of Canterbury could not easily be resisted. The change also held other attractions. His Oxford practice and researches had developed to such an extent that such a small city could scarcely occupy all his energies, and in London the medical and scientific community was considerably greater. His first publication in 1659 of *Diatribae*

Duae Medico-philosophicae had given him a reputation as an iatrochemist and many of his remedies were now sought, whilst the appearance of *Cerebri Anatome* in 1664 made him famous as an anatomist and brought in 1665 his honorary Fellowship of the Royal College of Physicians.

Undoubtedly his medical practice would be more lucrative, and for Willis, despite his great piety and philanthropy, this may have been an important consideration. In Oxford his medical fees were the highest and his income exceeded that of any person. In London he would expect a similar financial success.

In London, Willis took a large house with a coach house and stabling on the west side of St Martin's Lane. The location of the house is now obscured by tall buildings on both sides of a busy London street but an undated newspaper cutting in the City of Westminster Archives describes St Martin's Lane as 'first built between the years 1610 and 1615. Up to that time it was a green country lane, known as West Church Lane, with scarcely a single cottage all the way up to St Giles'.

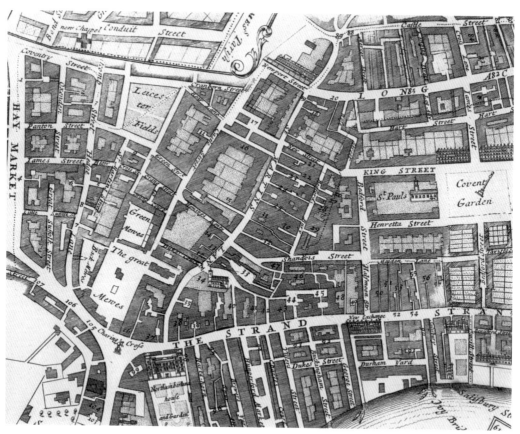

Detail of eighteenth century map of London showing St Martin's Lane running from the union of Newport Street and Long Acre down to the Strand. Rebuilding has destroyed any trace of Willis's house on the west side of St Martin's Lane. St Martin's church, which Willis attended, has also been rebuilt (Sutherland Collection, Ashmolean Library, University of Oxford).

As in Oxford, Willis instituted a daily routine of religious observance, mainly based on St Martin's Church. In the words of Thomas Birch[1],

> He rose early in the morning, that he might be present at divine service, (which he seldom or never failed) before he visited his patients, he agreed with the schoolmaster, who taught in the vestry room adjoining to the Church of St Martin's, to read prayers in that church at six in the morning and seven in the winter as well as five in the evening.

West prospect of the old St Martin's Church in the Fields, Westminster, from an engraving by George Vertue. The caption inserted by Browne Willis remembers the legacy of Willis to provide early Morning Prayers and late Evening Prayers at the Church (Sutherland Collection, Ashmolean Library, University of Oxford).

Soon after Willis's move to London he suffered many grievous family bereavements. In May, he had already buried his son Richard in Merton College Chapel, and after only a few weeks in London, his daughter Catherine died on 30 September, aged less than five years. She was buried in Westminster Abbey.

Willis's gravestone in the Central Aisle of the North Transept of Westminster Abbey
(Courtesy of the Dean and Chapter of Westminster).

Further personal grief was to follow. Both his wife, Mary, and later his son Thomas, developed active pulmonary tuberculosis. Willis was clearly distracted by these illnesses. When in 1669 Thomas developed a persistent productive cough which did not respond to the remedies of his father, he was sent to Montpellier for the winter and returned much improved and resumed his studies at Westminster School. However, the consumption of Mary, Willis's beloved wife, progressed. Willis proposed to leave London 'as the likeliest means to obtain the recovery of a person so dear to him as she was', but apparently Mary would not move, and on 31 October 1670, she died. So Willis found himself alone with the care of four young children, Thomas, Anne, Rachel, and Jane. Willis's grief drove him to great industry in his medical practice, scientific studies, and writing. His remarriage in 1672 to the widow Dame Elizabeth Calley partly filled the void left by the passing of his wife.

The Royal College of Physicians might have attracted Willis in London, but he seems to have been an infrequent visitor. His status in the College was unusual, in that he was one of the honorary fellows of the College, a category created to include doctors from the provinces, either country practitioners or university doctors, and, possibly incidentally, to bring in revenue. Munk's *Roll* gives the date of the election of Willis to an honorary fellowship as December 1665. The entrance fee was £20, much higher than the fees for candidature and licentiates. The Oath sworn by the Honorary Fellows indicated the limitation of their privileges, which did not include any important powers in the running of the College. They were, however, expected to contribute to the finances of the College and it seems their other obligations were much as the other fellows. It follows from this that Willis did not attend Comitia, as did several of his Oxford colleagues. The plague year was a difficult one for the College but even worse was to come with the Great Fire of London. The Book of Annals of the College records:

> On the 2nd of Sept a great fire broke out, unheard of before this time, in which well nigh the whole city and also the College itself, with the greater part of the library, burned.

Here may lie a practical explanation of why Willis had little to do with the College, which did not acquire suitable premises until some years after his death in 1675. It is puzzling however that Dr Willis did not apparently contribute to the rebuilding of the College. His name did not appear in the first subscription list made at Comitia at the house of Dr Stanley on 28 April 1669.

The Royal Society of London also saw little of Willis and this lack of contact of one who has been regarded as a founder requires comment. The matter is bound up with the early history of the Royal Society, the subject of much recent historical research. The early account by Bishop Thomas Sprat (1635-1713) and the later history by Thomas Birch (1705-1766) have now been cogently challenged. Many papers appeared in 1960 on the occasion of the tercentenary of the Society, and several of these writings analysed the medical contribution to the early membership. One article by Sir Charles Symonds specifically dealt with the contribution of Willis in the foundation.[2] Charles Webster has researched this subject extensively and I quote from him:[3]

> Sprat's description of the origins of the Royal Society in terms of the establishment of the Oxford Experimental Philosophy Club at Wadham by his patron John Wilkins, and its transference to London shortly before the restoration, is a severe distortion. The Club at Oxford was itself an offshoot of the London group, and it followed the same pattern of organisation. The two groups maintained a close association, until first Rooke and later Wren migrated to London.

My view formed from the many papers and articles quoted here, and my own researches described below, is that Willis was not a 'founder' of the Royal Society, except in so far as he was a prominent member of a group of Oxford scientists, many of whom moved to London and were active members of the Society from its beginnings. From the attendances at meetings of the Royal Society from December 1660-June 1663 (analysed by Webster), *Robert Boyle, Walter Charleton, Robert Hooke, William Petty, John Wilkins, and Christopher Wren* stand out as regular attenders at the first meetings of the Society who were close colleagues of Willis at Oxford. Willis is not included in the tables as his attendances were negligible.

Having dealt with a matter of controversy at some length, I shall mention such contacts of Willis with the Royal Society that may be found. The document entitled *The Signatures in the First Journal-Book and the Charter-Book of the Royal Society 1660-1679* is important in this context.[4] Thomas Willis appears at the bottom on the left of what is page 6 in the fascimile copy. On the same page appear the names of William Petty and Robert Boyle. On the previous page are the names of Robert Hooke, Ralph Bathurst, Walter Charleton, John Aubrey, and Christopher Wren, and on the subsequent page is the name of Richard Lower. Willis does appear on the list of proposed members dated 28 November 1660 but his name is *not* among the signatures of those present at what is termed the 'foundation meeting' on 5 December 1660. The papers of the Royal Society contain some references to Willis, notably contemporary reviews of his books in the *Philosophical Transactions*. Willis was asked to comment on certain powders obtained by the evaporation of 'Spaw Water' and replied in a letter dated 12 December 1667.

Willis's views on hysteria and hypochondria (see Chapter 9) had aroused criticism, notably from Nathaniel Highmore (1613-1685), in a publication directly attacking Willis, *De Hysterica et Hypochondriaca Passione Responsio Epistolaris ad Doctissimum Willisum*. In 1670 Willis replied in two essays, 'De sanguinis Accensione', and 'De Motu Musculari'. Dr Isler has ably reviewed this interesting controversy, the upshot of which was that Willis firmly adhered to his original opinion that hysteria was a disease of the nervous system.[5] Willis was now busy writing what would be published as *De Anima Brutorum* in 1672. The theme of this splendid book was 'psychologia', and its writing was undertaken after the death of his first wife Mary in 1670, 'that I might think the less of my grief'. Having written the anatomy of the brain in *De Cerebri Anatome* and its pathology in *Pathologiae Cerebri* he now wished to complete a trilogy with a book on the mental processes of the brain and their derangement. It was in effect an early work in psychiatry, but in its final form included neuroanatomy, comparative anatomy and many case reports. Willis now had great experience of anatomy of diverse species which included the earthworm, oyster, and the crayfish, and much of this work was now included in *De Anima Brutorum*. To help him in these dissections and in his medical practice had had two assistants Edmund King (1619-1709) and John Masters (1637-?) since in London, as in Oxford, Willis had assembled a small team of helpers. He also continued to employ his old Oxford apothecary John Hemmings and had retained in London the services of his coachman, Thomas Bush.

Willis's practice in London was now exceptionally large. Besides the poor, which he saw gratis, he had the medical care of the families of the wealthy London merchants, the important divines, the aristocratic families, and occasionally of Royalty. He was now physician-in-ordinary to Charles II and was consulted by the Duchess of York. This poor lady had suffered several miscarriages and borne some weakly infants which had not survived. Willis's famous opinion *'mala stamina vitae'* gave much offence and may have terminated his position as consultant to the Royal Family. Willis was not knighted, and possibly for this reason, although an eighteenth century biography states that he refused a knighthood.[6]

In 1672 Willis remarried and his new wife is described in Chapter 12. He was now wealthy and began to acquire property. He leased a large country mansion in Surrey for his new bride, who was accustomed to a large estate. This may have been intended as a temporary abode for, soon after, he leased a grand moated mansion, built by Henry I, the son of William the Conqueror. This was Ham Court in Chertsey, Surrey and situated on the south bank of the Thames. Willis was now in full flood of medical practice, scientific research and writing. The first part of *Pharmaceutice Rationalis* appeared in 1674, after which Willis began work on the second part, which proved to be his last writing task.

Willis, in the spring of 1675, proceeded to buy a large estate in Buckinghamshire from the Duke of Buckingham. This comprised three manors, one at Fenny Stratford, another at Great Brickhill, and one at Water Eaton. Why he purchased this extensive property is of interest. Having his Norman mansion in Surrey and his town house in St Martin's Lane, he could not have needed a place to live. Willis was always a property man and probably bought this large estate as an investment. He had been seriously ill in 1674 and this illness may have directed his thoughts to providing for his children. The details of this illness in 1674 are not known accurately but possibly Willis had pulmonary tuberculosis. His first wife and several of his children had died from this disease, from which his surviving son had recovered following a period in Montpellier. If this was the reason, Willis's prognosis was correct, since he died in November of the same year.

REFERENCES

1   Thomas Birch. *The History of Illustrious Persons of Great Britain, Engraved by Mr Houbracken, and Mr Vertue. With their Lives and Characters.* 2 Vols. London: 1743-1751.

2   Sir Charles Symonds. Thomas Willis. In: *The Royal Society Its Origins and Founders*, edited by Sir Harold Hartley. London: Royal Society, 1960.

3   C Webster. *The Great Instauration: Science, Medicine and Reform, 1626-1660.* London: Duckworth, 1975, p 93.

4   *The Signatures in the First Journal-Book and the Charter-Book of the Royal Society,* 4th edn. London: Royal Society, 1980.

5   H Isler. *Thomas Willis, 1621-1675: Doctor and Scientist.* Hafner, New York and London: 1968.

6   Notice on Thomas Willis. In: *Biographia Britannica*, Vol 6, Part 2. London: 1766.

Chapter 12

Willis's Family

I give unto every of my three daughters, Anne, Jane and Rachel the summe of £3,000 a peece

The Will of Thomas Willis[1]

There is every indication in Willis's life of his regard for the family. As a child he grew up in a loving caring home and the tragedy of the early death of his mother, Rachel, was repaired in part by the swift remarriage of his father to the recently widowed, Mrs Ruffin. As Mrs Ruffin brought three sons and two daughters to join Willis's two brothers and several sisters, Willis was accustomed to living in a large family. In his prosperous later life, he remained in touch with his brothers and sisters, whom he helped financially. His will made provision for his sister and her three children, and the five children of his surviving brother Thomas, who was a Fellow of Trinity College. His younger brother William Willis (1631-1662) had joined the group of scientists at Trinity College and had been a fellow at that college until his death in the autumn of 1662. His other younger brother was, according to Anthony Wood, 'one John Willis a good attorney, chapter clerk of Christ Church college who drew up all the leases &c of that college'.

The contemporary accounts of Willis confirm the impression of a devoted husband and father, limited by the demands of his work in the time he could spend with his wife and children. He was always praised for his attention to his patients and mention is made of distant visits into the country and ungrudging visits during what today we would term unsocial hours. His own family might have been large if he had not suffered the grievous early death of his first wife Mary and five of his nine children. The frequent occurrence of multiple deaths in a large family is not usual today in developed countries but in Willis's time these natural familial tragedies were commonplace and he would regularly see these numbers of deaths in the families of his patients. It remained a familiar background to life for over 200 years after Willis's time. In the mid-seventeenth century the family unit was remarkably strong. Some evidence for this is the facility of obtaining the records reproduced here of the births, baptisms, and deaths in Willis's family, 300 years ago. Today there is a profound change in the cohesion of a family, although, in the young, there is little serious morbidity, and excepting road accidents, little mortality. Yet, as I write, I hear that only one half of the children of the United Kingdom will begin their life and end their childhood with the same legal father and mother. Willis would have been astonished by this insecurity of family life and this lack of parental responsibility.

We have described earlier his mother Rachel who died in 1631 when Willis was a child of 10, just as he was beginning his schooling at Sylvester's Academy. His new stepmother, Magdalene, was to care for him during his time at day school and subsequently when he attended Christ Church.

Thomas Willis (father), died in June 1643, when Willis was 18 years old, and a year after he had proceeded to master of arts. His stepmother died 10 days after her husband and from the same cause. In 1643, Oxford was the Royalist headquarters of King Charles II and was excessively crowded, not only by the influx of the attendants of the King and his court, but also by the Royalist defenders of the city. The overcrowded city and many of the nearby villages were gravely affected by an epidemic fever. This fever affected both Parliamentary and Royalist forces and began when the Earl of Essex was commanding the parliamentary forces besieging the Royalist-held city of Reading. The fever spread to Oxford in 1643 and two of its victims were the father and stepmother of Willis. Although Willis was at the time only 18 years, he studied and described this epidemic, with such care, that it forms an early statement of an epidemic of fever. Although there are other possibilities, we generally recognise this disease, which afflicted Reading, Oxford, and the surrounding villages around Oxford, as the first recorded epidemic of typhus fever. The importance to this biography of the tragic deaths of Willis's father and stepmother are twofold. Willis at this early age became the head of two families comprising several young children, suddenly orphaned, and looking to him for support. The double tragedy and sudden family responsibilities must have discouraged any ambitions of a career in the church. This experience might have reinforced Willis's decision to take up medicine. A search for an explanation of this epidemic, which caused many deaths, including those of his father and stepmother, might have stimulated his enquiring mind. From his subsequent career, we may infer that he would not attribute the epidemic solely to divine intervention.

The first stages of Willis's career as a medical practitioner progressed slowly. He had no great patron and no established medical practice to inherit. It was 1657, still under the protectorate, and at the age of 36 years, when he felt able to support a wife. His chosen bride was Mary Fell who he had known for some time and probably their courtship had lasted several years. He was well known to her family and in particular to her brother John Fell (1625-1686). Mary Fell was the daughter of the Reverend Samuel Fell DD (1584-1649), by Margaret, daughter of Thomas Wylde Esq. Dr Samuel Fell is assured of a place in history from his strong championship of the Royalist cause in Oxford. On 24 June 1666 Sir Thomas Glenham had surrendered Oxford to General Fairfax but the city, dominated by the University, remained strongly Royalist. Samuel Fell, the Vice Chancellor and Dean of Christ Church was the leader of the 'resistance', which was terminated by a purge of leading Royalists begun by the Parliamentary Visitors in March 1648. Dr Fell was imprisoned and his family commanded to vacate the Deanery of Christ Church. Mrs Fell and her daughters proved resolute in mounting a determined resistance to their ejection. When, on the morning of 3 April 1648, the Provost Marshall accompanied the University Visitors to the deanery, they found the doors securely bolted. Even when the doors were broken and ingress obtained, the redoubtable Mrs Fell and her daughters refused to leave. According to the detailed account by Anthony Wood,[2] a guard was mounted in the house with instructions 'to weary her out with noise, rudeness, smell of tobacco etc.' These measures had failed to persuade these resolute ladies to depart after eight days, and forcible ejection was decided upon, described again by Wood:

> In the morn, the Chancellor, the Visitors, certain Soldiers and a great rabble of people went to Christ Church, where forthwith entering Dr. Fell's Lodgings (he being yet in safe custody at London) the Chancellor desired Mrs. Fell to quit her Quarters, telling her that in so doing she would do God and her Country good service: but she refusing that kind proposal, had very ill language first given to her by him, and then she was carried into the Quadrangle in a chair by soldiers. Her children also were carried out upon boards, as 'twas reported.

Willis at this time lived in Christ Church, and in rooms near the Deanery. He must have been a witness to the public ejection of the Fell's family and effects. It is quite likely that he saw his future wife, Mary, carried from the Deanery by soldiers in a chair.

John Fell (1625-1686), brother of Mary, became a lifelong friend of Willis. They were students together at University, although Willis was older by four years. Their great friendship probably began in the Civil War when, during the siege of Oxford, both served in the same regiment, raised by the Earl of Dover. A closer bond arose during the Protectorate. In 1648, at about the time of the ejection of the Fell family, described above, Willis decided to evade the puritan reforms of church services. Latin prayers were to be replaced by extempory prayer, in the vernacular, discarding the Book of Common Prayer. Vestments and all adornments of the church were discouraged and, indeed, much destruction of the interiors of churches took place. Willis invited certain loyal churchmen into his rooms in Christ Church, and subsequently to an 'oratory' created at his house, Beam Hall, where they performed religious services according to the traditional rites of the Anglican Church. John Fell was the leading churchman of this group and later spoke of his gratitude to Willis and his bravery at a difficult time for the Anglican Church. With the Restoration, the fortunes of John Fell changed. He became Dean of Christ Church, as had been his father, and in 1676 he was appointed Bishop of Oxford. His Deanship at Christ

St Michael's Church, where Willis married Mary Fell. Print from the Gentleman's Magazine, 1823

Church is memorable for his restoration of its buildings and encouragement of poor scholars and general improvement of academic standards. Today he is also remembered for the verses of Thomas Brown (1663-1704) beginning 'I do not love thee, Dr Fell'. In this biography, the obituary written by John Fell has proved useful in providing several statements about Willis's life and family.

The marriage of Thomas and Mary took place on 7 April 1657 at St Michael's at the North Gate, a small, but lovely church, still standing in Oxford and little changed today since the mid-seventeenth century.[3] It is now the oldest church in Oxford and probably Oxford's oldest building. It has a Saxon tower formerly incorporated into the wall of Oxford, and guarding the northern entrance to the city. The record of the marriage is now preserved in the Oxfordshire County Record Office, in Oxford. The groom is recorded as 'Willis Thomas Mr. Bachelor of Phisick of Christ-Church Oxford', and the bride as Fell Mary Miss. of Hereford, Herefords, spinster'. The officer recording the marriage appears as 'Richard Phillpott, J.P for Countie of Hereford', a justice of the peace from Hereford, as required by the puritan ordinances during the protectorate. Mr John Dolben, of York, and Mr Richard Allestree of Eton are said to have read the liturgy.

The married couple set up their home in Beam Hall, a house in Merton Street directly opposite Merton College. The house survives today as a substantial dwelling owned by Merton College, and occupied by their tenants. Some time before Willis's occupation, it had been one of the numerous small Halls of Oxford University. Willis maintained a large household in Beam Hall, to attend to his wife and his family, which, as he left for London, numbered five children. He maintained a coachman, who was essential to his large country practice. He also employed a valet, Thomas Bush, and three other servants. Another very important employee was his apothecary John Hemmings who, at Beam Hall, made up his prescriptions. This household was unusually large for an Oxford doctor at that time, and is evidence of the success of Willis's medical practice. Most Oxford doctors worked from rooms in their colleges.

The records of the births and deaths of the first eight children appear in the records of Merton College. The manuscript records were transcribed in the seventeenth century by the indefatigable Anthony Wood. They have been more recently edited by AJ Bott and published by Merton College in 1964 (burials)[4] and 1981 (baptisms and marriages).[5] In the extracts which follow, I have placed the additions by Wood within square brackets.

The first child of the Willises, a boy, was born on 26 January 1657/1658 and named Thomas, thus perpetuating the name of his father, grandfather, and great grandfather. He was baptised in the chapel of Merton College close to his home. The entry reads:

> 1657/8 Jan 26. THOMAS son of Mr. Thomas Willis a physitian & Mary [Fell] his wife, as borne in the great stone house against Mert. Coll church & afterwards bapt. in the p. [Ant a Wood].

Thomas, the first born, must have been a great joy to his parents, being their only surviving son. Thomas Willis (son, 1658-1699) moved with Willis to London where he attended Westminster School. His name does not appear in the list of alumni by Stenning (1928) but his attendance there seems not in doubt from the records of his son, Browne Willis. This first-born son suffered from chronic chest disease, diagnosed by his father as pulmonary tuberculosis. Willis sent his son to Montpellier in France in the hope that the warm climate of this Languedoc region near the Mediterranean Sea would cure his tuberculosis, and apparently with good effect. Willis wanted his wife Mary to take the cure of residence abroad. She declined to leave Willis and his family in London, and died, of tuberculosis, in London in 1670. Thomas Willis (son) attended Christ Church Oxford, the college of his father. He married in Westminster Abbey, on 20 May 1681, Alice the eldest daughter of Robert Browne of Dorset, from whom his first son took the name of Browne Willis.

The next child was a boy born on 20 June 1660 and named Samuel after his mother's father. The entry is as follows: '1660. June 20th. Samuel son of Dr. Thomas Willis & Marie his wife was borne and afterwards bapt in this par'.

Poor Samuel lived only a few months and his burial is recorded as follows: '1658 Samuel Willis an infant son of our Thos Willis a physician was buried in the north or parish isle'. The third child, a girl and named Mary after her mother, was born on New Year's Day 1662. The entry is as follows: '1661/2 Jan 1st. Mary dau of Mr [Dr] Thomas Willis & Mary his wife was borne [and afterwards bapt by Mr, John Wilton STB capellar chapleyme] Ant a Wood'. Mary lived only seven months dying on 1 September 1662. The entry reads: '1662 Sept 1st, Marie dau of Dr Tho Willis a phisitian died. Buried the same day in the parish part or Isle'. The death of the younger brother of Willis, William Willis (1631-1662) a few weeks later added to the tragedy felt by Thomas and Mary. The fourth child was a boy and again the name of Samuel was given. Samuel *secundus* lived only a few weeks dying on 11 April 1663. His burial record reads: '1663 April 11th. Samuel son of Dr. Thom Willis a physitian was buried in the north or parish part of the church'.

The next child, Catherine, was born on 5 February 1662/3, and the record of baptism reads: "Catherine [Katherine] (dau of Dr. Thomas Willis & Mary his wife was borne. Bapt. ye 17 day) [by Mr. John Wilton]'. Catherine survived the move of the Willis family to London in the summer of 1667 but died shortly after in London. She was buried in Westminster Abbey on 30 September 1667 in a grave where she was later joined by the remains of her mother and her father. The sixth child was Richard, born on 20 January 1663/4. The baptism record states: '1663/4 Feb. 2. Richard son of Dr Thomas Willis was bapt [by Mr John Wilton STB chapleyne] Borne 20 Jan going before'. Richard lived for three years and was buried in Merton, recorded thus: '1667 May 3. Richard Willis son of Dr. Tho Willis was buried in the north isle of this church'. The next two children were also born in Beam Hall and survived the move to London and, with the first born Thomas and the later Rachel, outlived their mother and father. Anne was born on 30 June 1665 and baptised on 7 July. The record states: '1665 July 7th Anne dau of Dr Thomas Willis was bapt. Borne 30 of June going before'. Jane was born in Oxford on 8 September 1666, and may have been the last of the children to be born in Oxford. Her record reads: '1666 Sept 14 Jane dau of Dr. Thomas Willis a physitian & Mary his wife was bapt. Borne the 8th day of the same month'. Rachel was the ninth and last child of Willis. Rachel was born in 1667, the year of the move to Oxford. She may not have been born in Beam Hall, since, alone of all the children, she does not appear in the records of baptisms of Merton College. Possibly she was baptised in London, but there is no record of this in the registers of Westminster Abbey.

Willis's second wedding took place on 1 September 1672 in Westminster Abbey.[6] His first wife, Mary, had died on 31 October 1670, leaving Willis with the four children, Thomas, Anne, Jane, and Rachel. His new bride was Elizabeth, eldest daughter of the Reverend Dr Matthew Nicholas (1594-

WILLIS'S FAMILY   103

1661), Dean of St Paul's by Elizabeth, daughter of William Fowke, of Bulwich, Northants. Elizabeth was the widow of Sir William Galley of Burderop Park, Wilts. Elizabeth was well connected and was the niece of Sir Edward Nicholas who had been Secretary of State to King Charles II. The marriage took place in Westminster Abbey on 1 September 1672. The records of the Abbey give their names as Dr Thomas Willis and Mrs Elizabeth Collier and elsewhere her name is misspelt as Cawly. Rightly her name was Dame Elizabeth Calley. Willis lived only three years after his second marriage. His widow survived him and remarried, her third husband being Sir Thomas Mompesson of Bathampton, Wiltshire, who died on 11 June 1701, and was buried in Salisbury. Willis's second wife died a widow on 29 November 1709 in her seventy-fifth year and was buried in Winchester Cathedral.

The medical aspects of the Willis family are of interest. The pattern of deaths in the family suggest that most and possibly all members of the family suffered from tuberculosis. The multiple deaths in childhood, but not in the immediate neonatal period, suggest to me that these children were born healthy, but subsequently developed the disease from which they died. My diagnosis in these early deaths would be *acute miliary tuberculosis* contracted from the parents and proving fatal in a child with little or no immunity to the disease. Probably the mother had chronic pulmonary tuberculosis, and the disease was likely to have caused apical cavities in the upper lobes of both of her lungs. This pulmonary pathology would be associated with chronic cough with the production of sputum containing abundant tubercle bacilli. Her children would be infected in the first weeks or months of their lives, and, having little or no immunity, would succumb. Willis himself diagnosed tuberculosis in his first wife and in his son, Thomas. It is possible that Willis himself had chronic pulmonary tuberculosis, although we have no clear evidence of this. His own death was due to an acute chest infection described by John Fell as follows:

> in the beginning of November he seemed troubled with a Cough (now the Epidemical Disease of the time) which (while it was thought light and inconsiderable) suddenly passed into a Pleurisie and Peripneumonia.

This was probably an acute bronchopneumonia but might have been a superadded bacterial infection on the basis of chronic phthisis. If he had chronic tuberculosis, his body would have been well adjusted to the infection. He had lived until his fifty-fourth year a life of unremitting labour.

I conclude this account of Willis's family with a short biographical sketch of his grandson, Browne Willis (1682-1760), who achieved fame as an antiquary. Browne Willis was a wealthy man throughout his life, having inherited large estates from his father, these being derived originally from the wealth of his grandfather. Browne Willis was born on 14 September 1682 at

Blandford St Mary. He attended Westminster School where it is said that his visits to the nearby Westminster Abbey as a schoolboy infused him with a love of antiquities, and cathedrals in particular. He proceeded to Christ Church, Oxford, but changed to study law at the Inner Temple in London. He owned Whaddon Hall in Buckinghamshire, the neighbouring manor of Bletchley, and the manor of Burlton in Burghill, Hertfordshire. From 1705-1708 he was member of parliament for the borough of Buckingham, his favourite town. He never practised law and after this brief experience of politics, devoted his life to the study of antiquities. He was especially interested in cathedrals and their histories which he studied from their records and registers. His surveys of four Welsh cathedrals, and 14 English cathedrals were published between 1717 and 1730. They form an important collection of data, but numerous inaccuracies of detail in these and other works have been discovered. Whilst historical research was his main preoccupation, Browne Willis had many other interests, including the collecting of manuscripts, books, pictures, and coins, most of which came, at his death, to the University of Oxford.

Browne Willis was very proud of his famous medical grandfather and took several actions to perpetuate his memory. On 7 March 1725 he wrote at length to Bishop Kennet obeying 'your lordship's commands in communicating something of my good grandfather Dr. Willis.' This detailed letter, reproduced in the 1814 edition of Anthony Wood's *Athenae Oxonienses* (Vol 3, pp 1048-1053), is an important source of biography used in this present work. Browne Willis visited his grandfather's birthplace in Great Bedwyn and examined the baptismal entry in the Parish Register of the church of St Mary the Virgin. He erased the entry below that of his grandfather and inserted the following: 'N.b. He was the most Famous Physitian in the World in his tyme & dying Nov. the 11th 1675 in the 54th year of his age, was buried in Westminster Abbey.' Browne Willis was fond of building and spent large sums on memorials and extensions to churches. His financial enterprises eventually exceeded his fortune and in later life he was forced to economise in his personal expenses, living in penury. To perpetuate the memory of Willis he was the prime mover in the construction of the church of St Martin's at Fenny Stratford in Buckinghamshire, near his home at Whaddon Hall. Browne Willis died at Whaddon Hall on 5 February 1760, and on 11 February was buried beneath the altar of the chapel in Fenny Stratford.

Browne Willis was instrumental in the choice of the dedication of this church in Fenny Stratford to St Martin, which again recalled his grandfather. Willis in London attended St Martin's church and also lived in St Martin's Lane, and, by coincidence, died on St Martin's Day, 11 November. Browne Willis gave a sum of money to endow the preaching of a sermon on St Martin's Day, or a Sunday near it, in the memory of his grandfather. This annual sermon has been delivered in this church ever since and on 11 November 1990, when I attended, the sermon was preached by the Bishop of Oxford. Browne Willis also remembered Willis in Oxford by causing a memorial tablet to Dr Iles and his pupil Willis to be erected in the Chapel of Christ Church, the Cathedral of Oxford.

For the biographical details in this chapter I have drawn substantially on the references given in the biographical foreword.

REFERENCES

1   Will of Thomas Willis, P.C.C. 118 Dycer. Proved in London, 24 November, 1675.

2   Anthony Wood. *The History and Antiquities of the University of Oxford*, Book 1, Vol 2, edited by John Gutch, Oxford: 1756, pp 563-564.

3   The record of Willis's marriage to Mary Fell, is kept at the Oxfordshire County Record Office, Oxford.

4   A Bott. *Burials at Merton College*. Oxford: Merton College, 1964.

5   A Bott. *Baptisms and Marriages at Merton College*. Oxford: Merton College, 1981.

6   JL Chester (Ed). *The Marriage, Baptismal, and Burial Register of the Collegiate Church or Abbey of St Peter, Westminster*, Vol 10. London: Harleian Society, 1876.

Chapter 13

The Death of Willis, his Grave, Will, and Descendants

And when this most expert Person was not relieved by frequent Bleeding and diligent taking of Remedies, himself perceived the Period of his Life to approach, (his Friends hoping better;) and after three days his Household affairs being settled, and having taken the Viaticum of the Holy Eucharist, and being received into the peace of the Church, he commended his pious Soul to God, having his senses entire to his last breath, and finished his most exemplary Life with the like Death.

John Fell 1675

The death of Willis came in 1675, at the age of 54 years, at the height of his powers as a physician and writer. In that year the first part of *Pharmaceutice Rationalis* was being published in Oxford. It was dedicated to the Royal College of Physicians, to which body Willis had been elected an honorary fellow in 1664. In the preface he acknowledged the help of his physician Dr King and Dr Masters. In November of 1675, Willis developed a bad cough, that soon grew into 'pleurisy and peripneumonia'. He died of this respiratory complex on 11 November, having been attended by Dr King. Dr King's and Willis's own knowledge of the prognosis of his illness was such that his nearest friends and relatives were summoned to his bedside, notably his brother-in-law, John Fell, and his son Thomas, both from Oxford. On the 10 November he added a codicil to his will making Philip Fell and John Hemmings his sole executors, and that day his signature was appended in a weak but legible hand. He then celebrated holy communion for the last time before his death on St Martin's day, 11 November.

Willis is buried in the Collegiate Church of St Peter, at Westminster, commonly called Westminster Abbey.[1-3] His grave is in the North Transept, an interesting area in a church abounding everywhere with interest. This burial area is near the present north door which in the reign of Richard II was the north entrance with a large porch called Solomon's Porch. At the beginning of the eighteenth century this stone work was completely replaced by a new design by Wren, Willis's old Oxford colleague, assisted by Dickenson, and further changes were made in the nineteenth century. The memorial character of the area changed with the burial there in 1778 of William Pitt, First Earl of Chatham and the North Transept is now called 'the Statesmen's Aisle'. Here you will find gravestones marking the actual burials of Fox (1806), Wilberforce (1833), Peel (1850), and Gladstone (1898), whilst there are memorials to Canning (1827),

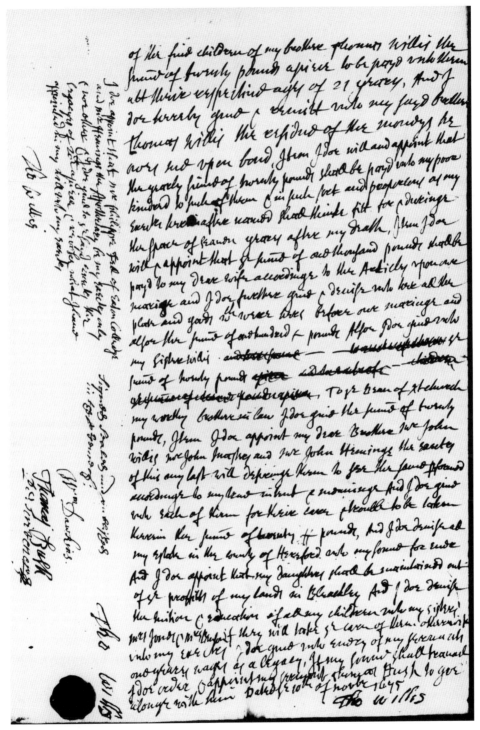

The Will of Thomas Willis, proved in London, on 24 November 1675. The last page is reproduced with the signed codicil added in the margin on the left on 10 November 1675, the day before Willis died (Public Record Office, London)

Cobden (1865), Palmerston (1865), Disraeli (1881), and Asquith (1928). There are many other graves and memorials.

Willis lies beneath the Central Aisle of the North Transept and his location is the nearest marked grave to the nave. With his burial, Willis joined the remains of his daughter, who was buried there in 1667, and Mary, his first wife, who was interred in the same grave in 1670. With the passage of time the grave was forgotten and its exact position became uncertain. William Feindel, of McGill University, Montreal, determined the position of the grave beneath a large floorstone measuring some 6 feet by 4 feet, and almost smooth, but identified by the letters 'Thos. Willis' in the lower right hand corner. A large transverse crack across the stone had probably been caused by the fall of the large central lantern from the roof in 1941. Feindel applied to the Royal College of Physicians of London and the Canadian Neurological Society for funds for the replacement of the stone, the new stone being cut, as had been the original, from black Belgian marble. The new memorial stone was dedicated on 1 September 1961, by the prayers of Canon Adam Fox, a laurel wreath being placed on the new stone by Sir Charles Symonds who made some fitting remarks to the assembly of neurologists, including Sir Russell Brain, then president of the Association of British Neurologists.

The inscription on the stone is in Latin of which the following is a translation:

> Mary, very dear wife of Thomas Willis, M.B. and also M.D., daughter of Samuel Fell, D.D. and Dean of Christ Church Cathedral, Oxford, a woman, if ever there was one, distinguished for piety, good sense, and sweetness of manners. She died to the great regret and grief of all, and especially of her husband, on the Eve of All Saints. A.D. 1670.
>
> And already there lies there, expecting the eternal daybreak of that feast, also in the same ground, Katherine, their daughter. She was buried on the day after Michaelmas, A.D. 1667.
>
> Here also lies the very celebrated Thomas Willis, M.D., aforesaid. He died November 11th, 1675, aged 54.

The news of Willis's death came to Oxford, in which city, his last work, the *Pharmaceutice Rationalis* was being printed. John Fell added a postscript which forms a valuable short obituary, frequently quoted in this biography. Further contemporary biographical accounts are given in Chapter 14.

Willis signed the codicil of his will on 10 November, the day before his death. His signature appears in several places, the last, the day before his death, then in a hand that, although legible, and recognisably his, seems to have been weak and tremulous. The will was proved in London on 24 November in the Prerogative Court of Canterbury, and the text is as follows.

In the Name of God, Amen. I, Thomas Willis, Doctor of Phisick, etc., do make my last will, etc. Imprimis I commend my soule, etc, My body I committ to the earth to be decently interred without any Pomp or Ostentation neere my wife and child in the Abbey Church at Westminster. My estate I dispose of in manner following. In the first place I do give, etc., unto the poore of the parish of St. Martins in the Fields the sum of £20 to be paid within a month after my decease and to be disposed of as the Rector of the said parish church for the time being shall appoint. Item, I doe give the yearely summe of £20 to be forever paid unto such person or persons being in Priests Orders as shall every morning and evening read the Common Prayer in the Parish Church of ST. Martins aforesaid as the same is now used. And my desire is that the Scholemaster of St. Martins aforesaid for the time being, if he shall be in Orders, shall doe the same. And if he shall not be in Orders, Then such person as shall be appointed thereunto by the Rector for the time being of the said Parish Church and the major part of the Gentlemen of the Vestry there. And I do hereby charge all my manors, lands, etc., which I lately purchased of his Grace the Duke of Bucks, in the County of Bucks, with the payment thereof. I do hereby will, etc., the said manners and lands unto my worthy freind Sir Lestrange Calthorpe, knight, his Majesty's Sergeant at Law, John Fell, D.D., Deane of Christchurch, George Benson, D.D., Dean of Hereford, John Willis, of the city of Oxford, gentleman, and John Hemings, of the parish of St. Martin in the Fields aforesaid, apothecary, their executors and assigns for the terme of 99 yeares upon trust for the payment of my debts and performance of my last will. And after the expiration, etc., of the said terme of 99 years. Then I doe devise the said Manners, &c., unto my onely sonn Thomas Willis and the heires of his body, and for want of such unto my right heires, but subject unto the payment of the said yearely summe of £20 for the reading of Prayers in St. Martins Church, as aforesaid, Provided that if Common Prayers according to the present Booke of Common Prayers established in the Church of England at this tyme shall not be used and read as I have directed them, my will, etc., is that the said yearely summe, etc., to cease and be void. Item, I give unto every of my three daughters, Anne, Jane and Rachell, the summe of £3,000 a peece, etc., to be paid unto them respectively at their several ages of 21 yeares or dayes of marriage, etc. Item, I doe devise, etc., unto my sister Phelp during her natural life the yearely sum of £40, and unto her daughter Mary the summe of £100, for a portion for her to be paid unto her at the age of 21 yeares, etc. And unto her two younger sonns to each of them the sum of £10 apeece. And I doe also give unto every of the fyve children of my brother Thomas Willis the sum of £20 apeece to be paid unto them at the respective ages of 21 yeares. ... Unto my said brother Thomas Willis the residue of the moneys he owes me upon bond. ... . The yearely sum of £20 shall be paid unto my poore kindred, etc., as my executore hereinafter named shall think fytt for and during the space of seaven yeares after my death. . . . £1000 shall be paid to my deare wife according to the articles upon our marriage. . . . Vnto her all the Plate and Goods which were hers before our marriage, and also the summe of £100 . . . Unto my sister Willis the summe of £20. ... To the Deane of Christchurch, my worthy brother-in-law, the summe of £20. Item, I doe appoint my deare brother, Mr. John Willis, Mr. John Masters and Mr. John Hemyngs the executors of this my last Will, desiring them to see the same performed according to my true intent and meaning. And I doe give unto each of them for their care and trouble to be taken therein the summe of £20. And I doe devise all my estate in the County of Hereford unto my sonn forever. And I doe appoint that my daughters shall be mainteyned out of the profitts of my lands in Bleakley. And I doe devise the tuition and education of all my children unto my sisters Mrs. Jones and Mrs. Benson if they will take care of them, otherwise my executors. I doe give unto every of my servants one yeares wages and a legacy. If my sonn shall travaile I doe order and appoint my servant, Thomas Bush, to goe along with him. Dated the tenth of November 1675.

Tho. Willis.

I doe appoint that Mr. Philipp Fell, of Eaton Colledg, and Mr. Hemyng, the Apothecary, be my executors only and no other. And I doe give unto the said Executors the Legacyes of £20 a peece. And revoke what I have appointed in my will unto my executors.

Tho. Willis.

Signed, sealed, and published in the presence of William Dawkins, Thomas Bush, Pe. Scrivener.

Willis was survived by a son, Thomas, and three daughters Anne, Jane, and Rachel. Thomas, his first born child, was born on 26 January 1657/1658 and his childhood and schooling have been described in Chapter 11. Briefly, he attended Westminster School and proceeded to Christ Church Oxford, the college of his father. He married in Westminster Abbey, on 20 May 1681, Alice the eldest daughter of Robert Browne of Dorset, from whom his first son took the name of Browne Willis.

Browne Willis was born on 14 September 1682 at Blandford St Mary, attended Westminster School, and Christ Church, Oxford, but changed to study law at the Inner Temple in London. He owned Whaddon Hall in Buckinghamshire, the neighbouring manor of Bletchley, and the manor of Burlton in Burghill, Hertfordshire. From 1705-1708 he was member of parliament for the borough of Buckingham. He never practised law and after this brief experience of politics, devoted his life to the study of antiquities. His books, papers, pictures and coins form an important acquisition of the University of Oxford. Further details of the life of Browne Willis are given in Chapter 12. He died at Whaddon Hall on 5 February 1760, and on 11 February was buried beneath the altar of the chapel in Fenny Stratford.

Browne Willis was instrumental in the choice of the dedication of the church in Fenny Stratford to St Martin, for the reason that it recalled his grandfather. Willis in London attended St Martin's church and also lived in St Martin's Lane, and, by coincidence, died on St Martin's Day, 11 November. Browne Willis gave a sum of money to endow the preaching of a sermon on St Martin's Day, or a Sunday near it, in the memory of his grandfather. This annual sermon has been delivered in this church ever since and on 11 November 1990, when I attended, the sermon was preached by the Bishop of Oxford.

Browne Willis also remembered Willis in Oxford by causing a memorial tablet to Dr Iles and his pupil Willis to be erected in the Chapel of Christ Church, the Cathedral of Oxford, and by presenting a portrait of Willis to the University.

REFERENCES

1   EW Brayley. *The History and Antiquities of the Abbey Church of St. Peter, Westminster*, Vol 2. London: Hurst Robinson and Co., 1823.
2   HF Westlake. *The New Guide to Westminster Abbey*, revised by LE Tanner. Oxford: AR Mowbray and Co., Ltd, 1960.
3   W Feindel. Restoration of memorial to Dr Thomas Willis (1621-75) in Westminster Abbey. *British Medical Journal*, 1962, Vol 1, pp 552-3.

Chapter 14

Portraits of Willis

He was middle statured: dark red hair (like a red pig):
stammered much

John Aubrey (1626-1697)

Several portraits of Willis exist and most of these are derived from one pictorial study of the subject. I have found several copies of the prints of one engraving, which first appeared in the various editions of his books,[1] another print in an early eighteenth century illustrated book of biographies,[2] and two surviving oil paintings.[3,4] The two prints have been reproduced innumerable times in various modern articles and books.

The likeness of Willis that has survived from a contemporary artist is the engraving of David Loggan. David Loggan (1635-1693 or 1700), was, from 1669, engraver to the University of Oxford, and his prolific but fine artistry has recorded the appearances of many Oxford persons, and much of Oxford architecture as it was in the seventeenth century. The Loggan print appeared as the frontispiece to *Pathologiae Cerebri,* facing the title (see p 55). This work was published in 1667 in Oxford by J Allestry. The engraving bears the signature 'D. Loggan delin. et Sculp', and the subscript gives the age of Willis as 45 years, and dates the work as 1666. The picture depicts Willis looking to the right, and includes the head and shoulders. The head and face suggest a powerful intellect with a broad brow, moderately high cheekbones, deep expressive eyes, a prominent nose, and a firm chin. We are fortunate in having this fine contemporary picture of Willis. Loggan was one of the most celebrated portrait engravers of his time, well known for his accurate portrayals, usually executed, as in this work, *ad vivum.* This print appeared in many of Willis's later works and further copies were engraved. A copy by Robert White (1645-1703), a pupil of Loggan, was made in 1685, and the frontispiece portrait of Willis in the Geneva edition of *Opera omnia* in 1694 was engraved by Isabella Piccini, again copying the Loggan engraving.

The other well known engraving of Willis was by the engraver and antiquary, George Vertue (1684-1756). It has been reproduced many times. Encircling Willis in the upper part of the spandrel is the title 'Thomas Willis M.D. obt.1675 Aeta 54'. Below, the print is inscribed 'G. Vertue Sculp 1742. in the possession of Browne Willis Esq. Impensis I & P Knapton Londinii 1742'.This engraving followed the Loggan print and possibly a painting or paintings were available to Vertue. It appeared in the two volume work of Thomas Birch (1705-1766), an English historian and biographer, and first appeared in 1743, being reprinted in 1756 and 1813. A short biography of Willis appears on pages 119-120 of Volume 1. The engraving by Vertue faces page 119.

Of the two known oil paintings of Willis, one hangs in the Lower Reading Room of the Bodleian Library, Oxford. It was painted by J Wollaston as one of a set of eight paintings of famous Oxford doctors of medicine, and formerly hung in the Department of Anatomy, the gift in 1735 of Humphrey Bartholomew. This fine oil painting, on canvas and measuring 30x25 inches, follows the details of Loggan's engraving. The portrait is half-length, threequarters to the right, and painted within an oval spandrel. Willis has brown hair, a small grey moustache, and is dressed in a black gown with a broad white collar.

The Royal College of Physicians possesses a portrait of Willis, on canvas and, measuring 29.5x24.5 inches, a size virtually the same as the Bodleian picture. This oil painting was purchased by the College in 1911, the previous history of the picture and the identity of the artist being unknown. The subject faces left (not right as in the Loggan and Vertue prints and the Bodleian painting) and is lit from the right. The left lower arm and hand are shown, holding a partly rolled paper inscribed 'Anatomy B . . .'. The face and dress are similar to the Loggan engraving and the Bodleian painting except for details of the tunic and collar.

Other paintings and drawings of Willis may exist but are not generally known. There is a record in the Register of Benefactions of the University of Oxford of a portrait of Willis given by the grandson Browne Willis in 1720, but this is not thought to be the painting in the Bodleian, described above.

REFERENCES

1 HJR Wing. A Bibliography of Dr Thomas Willis (1621-1675). Thesis, University of London, 1962.
2 Thomas Birch. *The Heads of Illustrious Persons of Great Britain, Engraved by Mr Houbraken, and Mr Vertue. With the Lives and Characters*, 2 Vols. London: 1743-1751.
3 RL Poole. *Catalogue of Portraits in the Bodleian Library*. Oxford: University Press, 1920.
4 G Wolstenholme. *The Royal College of Physicians of London: Portraits*. London: Churchill, 1964.

Chapter 15

Contemporary and Later Accounts of Willis

. . . what manner of person he was who wrote such things . . .
the matter requires a just commentary . . .

John Fell, 1675

John Fell (1625-1686), schoolfellow, brother-in-law, and lifelong friend, would be likely to say well of Willis, but it is of interest which plaudits he chooses.[1] Of Willis's period in Oxford he remarks:

> ... he proceeded Doctor, and was publickly declared Professor of Natural Philosophy, which Profession he did adorn with the highest praise.

Of Willis's move to London, Fell writes:

> But about the Year 1667, being called to London to practise Physick, it is incredible to relate, how soon, and with how great commendations he grew famous, especially being so composed by Nature and Custom, that he could not recommend himself by words composed to deceive, or the cunning Arts of Mountebanks.

Fell would deduce the medical reputation of Willis from the opinion of Willis's professional colleagues, but his appraisal of Willis as a man, would be from his own judgement, which he summarised thus:

> . . . how undisturbed he was in Adversity, and how temperate in Prosperity; how modest in the highest Fame for his Learning; when unworthily provok'd, how prone to forgive injuries; how faithful to his Prince to his death; how obedient to the oppressed Church; how candid and ingenuous in the Profession of his Art; how indefatigable in his Studyes, how sparing in his Speech, and how much a Christian in the whole state of his Life.

John Aubrey (1626-1697) a contemporary, and neighbour, who knew Willis well, and might have written a valuable biography, included only a few works in his description of Willis, published posthumously, and these were factual rather than an opinion by Aubrey on the life of Willis.[2] We read of his progress as a doctor that 'He grew more and more into good practice', and 'He studied chemistry in Peckwater Inn chamber. He was in those days very mathematical, and I have heard him say his genius lay more to mathematics than to chemistry.'

Henry Stubbe (1632-1676) dedicated his book *The Miraculous Conformist* 'To his very worthy and Learned Friend Dr. Thomas Willis, Doctor in Physique, and Professor of Natural Philosophy in Oxford', an interesting indication of friendship since it was Stubbe who first voiced the erroneous opinion that Richard Lower, and not Willis, had been the major composer of *Cerebri Anatome*.

Anthony Wood knew Willis very well and for many years was his neighbour, as Willis lived in Beam Hall and Wood lived in the adjoining Postmasters Hall. Consequently, Wood's opinion on Willis is of considerable interest, the more so as Wood was critical of Willis and indeed of many of the subjects of his biographical studies.[3] Wood wrote as follows:

> The truth is, tho' he was a plain man, a man of no great carriage, little discourse, complaisance or society, yet for his deep insight, happy researches in natural and experimental philosophy, anatomy, and chymistry, for his wonderful success and repute in his practice, the natural smoothness, pure elegancy, delightful, unaffected neatness of Latin stile, none scarce hath equall'd, much less out-done him, how great soever. When at any time he is mention'd by authors (as he is very often) it is done in words expressing their highest esteem of his great worth and excellency, and placed still, as first in rank, among physicians. And further also, he hath laid a lasting foundation of a body of physic chiefly on hypotheses of his own framing.

Richard Lower was the pupil and lifelong friend of Willis and succeeded to his practice in London. Lower always spoke and wrote of Willis with affection. The most tangible evidence of his esteem was his 1665 pamphlet *Diatribae Thomas Willis* ... in which he defended Willis from the criticism of Edmund O'Meara, a Bristol physician of Irish origin, who attacked Willis's publication *Of Fevers* ....

Of practising physicians, neurologists, in company with neuroscientists, have been the most vociferous in their praise. William Osler was critical, but had he read Willis with more care, he might have introduced myasthenia gravis into his own textbook. Russell Brain described Willis as 'The Harvey of the Nervous System'. Sir Charles Symonds was a champion of Willis as an anatomist, physiologist and physician. In a contribution to a work on the founders of the Royal Society, he praised not only his anatomical studies but also his work as a physician as follows:

> The fame of Willis, however, rests not only on his achievements as a professional anatomist. His observations on the natural history of disease were accurate and many of them original, and in his deductions, especially those derived from his anatomical knowledge he showed true imaginative genius.

Symonds was also impressed with Willis as a man for he concludes:

> As a man he was not a courtier but a pious industrious person whose medical practice was informed by the search for truth and whose success

as a doctor must be attributed as much–perhaps more–to the honesty and warmth of his character as to his skill.

Charles Sherrington (1857-1952) spoke for neurophysiologists thus, 'Willis put the brain and the nervous system on their modern footing, so far as that could then be done'.[4] The late Alfred Meyer found many original anatomical observations in the works of Willis but his most telling comment was that Willis in *Cerebri Anatome* had written the first monograph devoted exclusively to the brain, spinal cord, and peripheral nerves.[5]

We close with some comments from medical historians interested in Willis. Fielding H Garrison, the American medical historian, summarised Willis's achievements in these words:

> Willis was, like Sydenham, Heberden, and Bright, a remarkable example of the capacity of the English physicians for close, careful clinical observation.[7]

Kenneth Dewhurst who researched Willis for many years wrote, 'Outwardly pious, modest and unassuming, Thomas Willis was essentially a tireless, bold and speculative genius'.[7] Hasruedi Isler has reviewed Willis's work in detail and his judgement is too lengthy to be quoted here. Isler remarked that:

> Willis was an exceedingly gifted gatherer of data about ill and healthy Man. He was, one might say, possessed with the need to bring them into contex. He did this with the help of the scientific methods of his time, to which he contributed some notable advances.[8]

Robert G Frank, Jr has studied extensively the period during which Willis was in Oxford. In a short biography,[9] Frank concludes:

> Willis accomplished much, not in spite his penchant for speculation, but because of it. He attempted, with an energy and insight unsurpassed in the seventeenth century, to construct a medical system that encompassed not only his own anatomical discoveries and acute clinical observations, but set them within the emerging Harveian physiology and the new corpuscular natural philosophy.[10]

REFERENCES

1 John Fell's Postscript to *'Pharmaceutice Rationalis'*, Part 2. London: 1675. This was translated by S Pordage. In: *'Dr Willis's Practice of Physic'*. London: 1684. It appears as three unnumbered pages after the Preface to the Reader.
2 John Aubrey, *Brief Lives Chiefly of Contemporaries, Set Down by John Aubrey 1699-1696*, Vol 2, edited by Andrew Clark. Oxford: 1898, pp 302-4.

3   Anthony Wood, *Athenae Oxoniensis*, Vol 3, edited by Philip Bliss. 1817, pp 1048-53.

4   C Sherrington. *Man on his Nature*. Cambridge: 1951, p 194.

5   A Meyer. *Historical Aspects of Cerebral Anatomy*. London, New York, Toronto: Oxford University Press, 1971.

6   FH Garrison. *An Introduction to the History of Medicine*, 4th edn. Philadelphia and London: Saunders, 1929.

7   K Dewhurst. *Thomas Willis's Oxford Lectures*. Oxford: Sandford Publications, 1980.

8   H Isler. *Thomas Willis, 1621-1675: Doctor and Scientist*. Hafner, New York and London: 1968.

9   Frank RG Jr. Thomas Willis. In: *The Dictionary of Scientific Biography*, Vol 14. 1970-1976, pp 404-9.

Chapter 16

A Personal Appraisal of Willis's Life and Work

Honour a physician with the honour due to him
for the uses which ye may have of him:
for the Lord hath created him

Ecclesiasticus, XXXVIII, 1

David Loggan, the most famous portraitist of the seventeenth century, drew Willis from life. Looking at this study, one can see how Loggan discerned in his sitter a profound intellectual power, since this painter was interested in much more than the outward features of his subjects. Willis was not impressive on first acquaintance as we know from the comments of John Aubrey, 'middle statured' and 'stammered much', and of Anthony Wood, 'he was a plain Man, a Man of no Carriage, little Discourse, Complaisance or Society'. Willis was a shy man, who never sought fame or looked for high office, and throughout his life seemed content to be judged by the quality and quantity of his work. Willis was pious, charitable, and intensely loyal to his family and friends. His great industry was evident in all these attributes.

His piety was remarkable, and was seen in his daily routine, in his relations with his family and friends, and in his attendance on his patients. His church-going was as regular as a priest, and he celebrated the traditional Anglican services almost every day of his adult life. Had Willis been shipwrecked on a desert island, his first act would have been to thank Almighty God for his deliverance, whilst his second would have been to arrange for divine service to be celebrated every morning and evening. To his patients he interpreted any alleviation of their illnesses to divine intervention, his own part being that of a servant of God.

His charity had no significant bounds, and dated from his schooldays, when he would give away his packed lunch to the poor. He was generous with his time and wealth to his church, his family, and his friends, and his motive in making money seemed to be to assist others. He made gifts and bequests to several churches, to his family, and to his friends. He worked harder on Sunday than on a weekday, saw more patients, and gave all the fees from Sunday work to the poor, the amount being a tenth of his income. He attended to the medical care of the poor by seeing them, without fee, every morning after his church attendance and before his 'rounds' of his wealthy patients.

His loyalty was beyond question, to his family, friends, colleagues, and King. It seems as though once he had given his allegiance to a person, an institution, or a cause it was never withdrawn. His sympathies to the King and the Royalists came from the heart, as intellectually he was more in tune with the puritans, from whom so many of the innovations in science were proceeding. In these challenges posed by modern science to accepted beliefs, he was a willing participant, whilst, throughout his life, he never changed the form of his religious observance.

His industry was limited only by the length of the day, for usually he worked every day of the week, and every week of the year. Both at school and at university, his close attention to study was remarkable, and during the siege of Oxford he was conspicuous among the soldiery for his attempts to continue his studies. As a doctor he saw many patients, and one source alludes to 1000 in a week. In his practice he frequently travelled far from Oxford, first on horseback and later by coach. In his medical and scientific work, his talent for organisation multiplied the fruits of his talents. His great industry and his ability to attract and inspire his pupils in research work explains the great body of scientific work with which he was associated.

As a scholar, Willis was well read, both in the classics, and in contemporary works, which his wealth enabled him to purchase. He was a good Latinist, writing with accuracy and speed, and with such clarity that his descriptions of the illnesses of his patients can be translated into modern case reports. From this scholarship came the steady production of valuable books, which sold well, went into many editions and brought Willis fame in England and abroad. His works were used extensively in tuition throughout the world. He was much quoted and his fame brought him an international correspondence.

As a doctor Willis was caring and practical, but also innovative and observant. His care was evident in his attention to his patients, for whom he rose early and retired late, often having to travel long distances to see them, on first and several subsequent visits. His remedies were practical and based on common sense and personal experience as much as to the strange nostrums used in those times, many of which, however, were in his own pharmacopoeia. At that time hardly any disease had a specific remedy and Willis would include many traditional remedies, which were mainly derived from the great variety of medicinal herbs used. He was innovative with possible new remedies, particularly those compounded from inorganic chemistry. He investigated the chemical basis for the reputed medicinal value of healing springs. In treatment he followed the teaching of Paracelsus and Helmont, being against violent purging, blistering, and bleeding, so common at that time and for long afterwards, as, for example, in the fatal apoplexy of Charles II in 1685. The restraint and common sense of his remedies were probably the secret of his large successful practice in Oxford and in London, where his medical opinion was so commonly sought. His descriptions of patients give evidence of his careful observation of the symptoms and signs of his cases, these being observed throughout the illness. This power of observation coupled with profound study of the disease which he was observing was the great strength of Willis's work. At a time when diseases were considered to be varying manifestations of one disorder, Willis, from intense study of many cases of his immense practice, could see the pattern of a specific disease hitherto not recognised as a distinct entity. The importance of these clinical observations was magnified by his habit of performing necropsies on his cases, thus recognising the pathological basis for several diseases.

Willis had all the attributes of a notable scientist, not only in his personal work, but also in his talent for inspiring others. His keen enquiring mind, receptive to new ideas, and preferring direct observation, led to his achievements in anatomy, comparative anatomy, physiology, pathology, and medical science.

As an anatomist Willis began his studies at a stage when the revolution in anatomy was over, and for him anatomy according to Galen was never part of his education. His great vision was to recognise the need for a study of the anatomy of the nervous system. Thus his overall description of the anatomy of the brain, the spinal cord, and the peripheral and autonomic nervous system was a notable advance.[1] He made several important discoveries of which the description of the accessory nerve and of the ophthammic branch of the trigeminal nerve were entirely original. His description of the cerebral arterial circle, and its importance in physiology and clinical medicine amply justify its universal name of Circle of Willis. His work in comparative anatomy was immense and its analysis is beyond the scope of this book. At that time few animals had been 'anatomised' by such an expert as Willis and many original observations awaited description. Willis was interested in the similarities and differences between the anatomy of animals and humans but his curiosity was far wider than this practical help to the study of human anatomy. His dissections and descriptions of the structure of the earthworm, oyster, and crayfish are examples of his attention to the anatomy of all living creatures.

My opinion of Willis as a physiologist is that he was more constructive by his theories and his suggestions to others, than by his own experiments, much as he encouraged the experimental approach to science and medicine. Later in his career his attention to the patients in his practice concentrated his energies on human anatomy and human diseases. Earlier he did perform many animal experiments, but those of others, for example of his pupil Richard Lower, were more numerous and more productive of important scientific discoveries. Willis's theories of physiology, however, have an extraordinary prescience. Because he was addicted to speculation about subjects where facts were few, he often put forward a theory, for which he had no evidence, but which is now seen to be correct. An example is his suggestion that substances from glands may travel *via* the blood stream to exert an influence elsewhere, a prescient description of the action of the endocrine glands. These instances of accurate speculation are often quoted but we must allow that the few accuracies are submerged in a sea of other theories which so far remain absurd. Finally Willis's liking for order led him to gather up anatomical and physiological facts into systems, a most helpful concept in his time.

Willis has no reputation as a pathologist, yet the study of his works show him to be a pioneer in the explanation of disease states in the pathological anatomy found at necropsy. Elsewhere I have, from an analysis of his cases with necropsy, shown Willis to be the first neuropathologist in the world, to which he has bequeathed, in his works, a plethora of significant case reports discriminately examined at necropsy.[2] His fame as a neuropathologist exceeds that of others because of the wealth of his material, its rigorous pathological examination, and his custom of correlation of pathological with clinical findings, the latter being usually derived from his observations in his own medical practice.

In medical science Willis will always be remembered as a discoverer of new diseases, for example, achalasia of the cardia, akathisia, and myasthenia gravis. Organised, industrious, meticulous, enquiring, and observant are good qualities for a scientist, but Willis, as a man and a doctor, was also pious, loyal, and caring. His huge medical practice became a thesaurus of critically observed and recorded medical cases, on which his fame will endure.

As a teacher, Willis was one of the foremost figures in the new science movement in Oxford in the second half of the seventeenth century. One reason was his long period in Oxford, since many of the new scientists were more transient figures, moving away for career or family reasons. Willis's chair of Natural Philosophy was an excellent position for both his teaching and his scientific research. It also allowed him to develop a series of lectures on his findings and theories of anatomy, physiology, and pathology. These lectures were very popular, being well attended, not only by students of medicine and science, but also by other students in Oxford, often those whose career was in divinity. We know the content of Willis's lecture course from several contemporary comments, but also from the notebook of John Locke. The lectures were the basis of Willis's successful books, which spread his teaching throughout the world.

Willis was an excellent business man, as highly organised in the commercial aspects of his medical practice, as in his attention to his patients and pupils, and the conducting of his scientific research. He charged high fees, the highest in Oxford, and subsequently the highest in London. His medical work was assisted by deputies and this assistance multiplied his involvement with cases. He employed a personal apothecary, living in his house, to make up his prescriptions, and a coachman to take him on his rounds. He also had a doctor's office in his house, Beam Hall, to see patients and he later expanded his facilities by taking extensive premises in Oxford for this purpose and also probably to care for patients in what was effectively a small hospital. This organisation of medical practice was unusual at that time and explains not only the abundance of his clinical experience but also his financial success. At Oxford his income was greater than any other person in the city, and when he moved to London he built up, in the neighbourhood of Westminster, the first large medical practice in London. Anthony Wood wrote 'in very short time after he became so noted, and so infinitely resorted to, that never any physician before went beyond him, or got more Money nearly than he'. On his death this practice devolved on his pupil Richard Lower, and from him passed to John Radcliffe, whose fortune eventually provided the many Radcliffe bequests, mainly in Oxford.

The final judgement of history on Willis is incomplete, and this work is intended to illuminate some unknown or forgotten details of his life and work. How Willis rates as a seventeenth century scientist and doctor is a question that can only be answered by a personal opinion.

As a pure scientist, for example, in the subjects of inorganic chemistry or physics, I do not rate him highly. He was interested in these subjects which were then at an embryonal stage, but none of his minor discoveries have survived as an important contribution to knowledge. His colleague Robert Boyle was far more innovative and went on to a great career in science, as did Robert Hooke the pupil of Boyle.

As a medical scientist, the reputation of Willis rises to somewhere near the first place in the seventeenth century. A large body of important work in anatomy, some in the new subject of physiology, and a great deal, and possibly his major contribution, in clinical medicine, is formidable evidence of his pre-eminence as a medical scientist. We must concede that William Harvey surpasses Willis in distinction by a large margin, but this Harvey does in comparison with any doctor in any century.

REFERENCES

[1]   JT Hughes. Spinal cord arteries described by Willis, Chap 20. In: *Historical Aspects of the Neurosciences*, edited by FC Rose and WF Bynum. New York: Raven Press, 1982.

[2]   JT Hughes, Thomas Willis: the first Oxford neuropathologist. In: *Neuroscience Across the Centuries*, edited by FC Rose. London: Smith-Gordon, Niigata, Nishimura: 1989, pp 87-96.

Bibliography

I am indebted to the work of Mr HJR Wing (1962) for the earlier part of this bibliography.

Willis's own works
Details of these are given in Chapter 7.

1. *Diatribae Duae Medico-philosophicae*, 1659
2. *Cerebri Anatome*, 1664
3. *Pathologiae Cerebri*, 1667
4. *Affectionum Quae Dicuntur Hystericae et Hypochondriacae*, 1670
5. *De Anima Brutorum*, 1672
6. *Pharmaceutice Rationalis*, Parts I-II 1674-1675; Part II was published posthumously
7. *A Plain and Easie Method for Preserving Those That are Well from the Plague*, 1691 (posthumously)

Other publications in the seventeenth century
Aubrey, J. *Brief Lives, Chiefly of Contemporaries Set Down by John Aubrey Between the Years 1669 and 1696*. Vol 2, edited by Andrew Clark. Oxford: 1898. The short biography of Willis is on pp 302-4.
Bacon, Francis. *On the Advancement and Proficiency of Learning*, translated by Gilbert Watts. Oxford: 1640.
Bacon, Francis. *The New Atlantis*, edited by GC Moore Smith. Cambridge: Cambridge University Press, 1900.
Barbatus, H. *De Sanguine et Eius Sero, in Qua Procter Varia Lectu Dignissima, . . . Willisii Sued Nervorum Vis. . . Rancofurti ad Moen*. 1667. Willis is referred to on pp 22-4 and 72-4.
Barner, J. *Prodromus Sennerti Novi seu Delineatio Novi Medicinae Systematis, in Quo Quicquid a Primis Seculis in Hunc Usque Diem de Arte Prodiit,... Willisii,... Dogmata ex Principiis Anatomico-chymicis Examinantiur*. Augusta Vindelicorum, 1674.
Browne, Sir Thomas. *The Works of Sir Thomas Browne*, edited by G Keynes, 4 Vols. London: 1964.
Cassinus Conlo (pseudonym of Edmund de Meara). *Willisius Male Vindicatus Sive Medicus Oxoniensis Mendacitatis & Inscitiae Delectus*. Dublini: 1667.
Charleton, Walter. *Inquisitiones 11. Anatomico-physicae: Prior De Fulmine;*

Altera De Proprietatibus Cerebri Humani. Londonii: 1665. Willis is referred to on pp 57-141.

De la Pont, Charles. *Dissertationes Duae Medicae De Veneo Pestilenti, in Quarum Priore Agitur De Veneni Pestilentis Natura & Causuis Absque Ullo Occulatarum Qualitanem Figmento, Ubi Etiam D. Thomae Willisii de Veneni Pestilentis Natura Opinio Examinatur, & Ostenditur Venenum Pestilens Nulla Coagulandi sed Corrodendi vi Esse Praeditum* .... Amstelodami: 1671.

De Meara, Edmund. *Examen diatribae Thomas Willisii Doctoris Medici & Professoris Oxoniensis, De febribus.* Londinii: 1679.

Evelyn, John. *The Diary and Correspondence of John Evelyn FRS*, new edn, edited by William Bray, 4 Vols. London: 1854.

Evelyn, John. *The Diary of John Evelyn*, edited by ES de Beer, 6 Vols. Oxford: 1955.

Fell, John. Short obituary of Willis added as a postscript to the second part of Willis's *Pharmaceutie Rationalis* . . ., part 2. London: 1684.

Hannemann, Johannes Ludovicus. *Aetiologica Philosophico-medica Curiosa Facultatis Purgatricis qua Ostenditur Contra Willisium & Willisianos in Resinosis Particulis non ese Collocandam Catharsin.* .... Hamburgi: 1677.

Harris, Walter. *Pharmacologica Anti-empirica* .... London: 1683. This gives Willis's preparation on pp 149-53.

Harvey, Gideon. *The Conclave of Physicians* .... London: 1683. Chapter XVI on pp 185-203 has the subject 'Willis, his hypothesis of Agues is ridiculously erroneous'.

Highmore, Nathaniel. *De Hysterica & Hypochondrica Passione, Responsio Epistolaris ad Doctorem Willis Medicum Londiniensem Celeberrimum.* Londinii: 1670.

Lower, Richard. *Diatribae Thomas Willisii Doct. Med. & Profess. Oxon. De Febribus vindicatio Adversus Edmundum De Meara Ormoniensem Hibernum MD* .... Londinii: 1665.

Maynwaring, Everard. *Morbus Polyrhizos & Polymorphaeus. A Treatise of the Scurvy, . .. Traversing some Hypotheses of Dr. Willis Upon the Scurvy.* .... London: 1669.

Microscopium Hippocraticum, Sive Judicum de Umbris Haevei, Novae Medicinae Principis, Pequeti, Willisii, Procerum Illius, et De Motu Sanguinis in Animalibus .... Londinii: 1684.

Neues Liecht vor die Apothecker, wie selbige nach den Grund-Regeln der heutigen Destillirkunst ihre Artzeneyen zubereiten sollen; mit einigen Anmerckungen vermehret und verbessert durch die hochgelahrten Herren Sylvius, Willis, Blanchart, und anderer. . . . Leipzig: 1690.

Plot, Robert. *The Natural History of Oxfordshire.* Oxford: 1677. Willis is referred to on pp 301-5.

Portius, Lucas Antonius. *Erasistratus sive De sanguinis missione.* ... Venice: 1683. This work was concerned with venesection, which was discussed in the form of dialogues between Erasistratus, Galen, Willis, and van Helmont.

Reviews of Willis's works in the *Philosophical Transactions of the Royal Society*. Pathologiae cerebri & nervosi generis specimen, 1667, Vol 2, pp 600-2; Affectionum quae dicunter hystericae & hypochondricae pathologia spasmodica vindicata, 1670, Vol 5, p 1178, 1670; De anima brutorum, 1672, Vol 7, pp 4071-3; Pharmaceutice rationalis (Pars prima) 1673, Vol 8, pp 6166-6171; Pharmaceutice rationalis (Pars secunda), 1675, Vol 10, pp 505-9.

Salmon, W. *Iatrica: Seu Praxis Medendi. The Practice of Curing: Being a Medicinal History .... Together With Several of the Choicest Observations of Other Famous Men: Taken From .... Willis, and Several Others ....* London: 1681.

Sprat, T. *The History of the Royal Society of London, for The Improving of Natural Knowledge.* London: 1667.

Thomson, George. *Aimatiasis: or. The true Way of Preserving the Bloud in its Integrity and Rectifying it, if at Anytime Polluted and Degenerate: Wherein Dr Willis his Erroour of Bleeding is Reprehended, and Offered to be Confuted by Practice and Frequent Experiments ....* London: 1670.

Tilingius, Matthias. *Disquisitio Physico-medica De Fermentatione, sive De Motu Intestine Particularum in Quovis Corpoere, ex Fundamentis Willisianis & Moebianis in Philatrorum Gratia Adornata .... Atque in Certas Quaestiones Efformata, ...* Bremae: 1674.

Watkins, Richard. *Newes from the Dead: or a True and Exact Narration of the Miraculous Deliverance of Anne Greene, who Being Executed at Oxford Decemb. 14. 1650. Afterwards Revived; and By the Care of Certain Physitians There, is Now Perfectly Recovered.* Oxford: 1651. The 'certain physitians' were William Petty and Thomas Willis.

Wood, Anthony. *Athenae Oxonienses .... to Which are Added the Fasti*, edited by Philip Bliss, 4 Vols. London: 1813-1820. Willis is referred to in Vol 3, in columns 1048-53.

Eighteenth century publications

Barchusen, JC. *Historia Medicinae.* Amsterdam: 1710. This work is cast in the form of dialogues. Dialogus XVII is entitled 'De hypothesibus Tackenii, Sylvii, Willisii'.

Biographica Britannica, 6 Vols. London: 1747-1763. Willis is referred to in Vol 6 on pp 4291-7.

Birch, Thomas. *The Heads of Illustrius Persons of Great Britain, Engraved by Mr Houbracken, and Mr Vertue. With their Lives and Characters*, 2 Vols. London: 1743-1751. Willis appears in Vol 1 on pp 119-20. His portrait was engraved by Vertue.

Birch, Thomas. *The History of the Royal Society of London for Improving of Natural Knowledge, From its First Rise*, 4 Vols. London: 1756-7.

Eloy, NFJ. *Dictionnaire Historique de la Medecine Ancienne et Moderne . . .*, 4 Vols. Mons: 1778. Willis is referred to in Vol 4 on pp 577-9.

Freind, John. *The History of Physick . . .*, 4th edn, Part 11. London: 1710. The views of Willis on the function of the cerebrum and cerebellum are referred to on pp 315-17.

Granger, J. *A Biographical History of England from Egbert the Great to the Revolution . . .*, 3rd edn, Vol 4. London: 1779. Willis is referred to on pp 9-10.

Haller, Albrech von. *Bibliotheca Anatomica . . .*, Tomus 1. Tiguir: 1774. Willis's anatomical works are described on pp 475-7.

Haller, Albrech von. *Bibliotheca medicinae Practicae ...*, Tomus 111. Basileae: 1779. Willis's medical works are described on pp 73-7.

Hutchinson, Benjamin. *Biographia Medico...*, Vol 11. London: 1799. Willis is referred to on pp 481-5.

Manget, JJ. *Bibliothecae Scriptorum Medicorum...*, Tomus 11, Pars 11. Geneva: 1731. Willis is referred to on pp 618-20.

Niceron, Jean Pierre. *Mémoires pour Servir à l'Histoire des Hommes . . .*, Tome XV. Paris: 1731. Willis is referred to on pp 343-9.

Northcote, William. *A Concise History of Anatomy ....* London: 1772. Willis's contributions to anatomy are described on pp 123-4.

Portal, Antoine. *Histoire de l'Anatomie et de la Chirurgie*, Tome 111. Paris: 1770. Chap IV on pp 88-105 deals with Willis.

Senac, JD. *Traité de la Structure du Coeur, de son Action et de ses Maladies*, Tome 1. Paris: 1749. Willis's description of the innervation of the heart is given on pp 119-21.

Slare, Frederick. *Experiments and Observations upon Oriental and other Bezoar-stones, which Prove Them to be of No Use in Physick ... To Which is Annex'd a Vindication of Sugars Against the Charge of Dr Willis, other physicians, and common prejuices. . . .* London: 1715.

Stolle, Gottlieb. *Anieitung zur Historie der medicinischen Gelahreit*. Jena: 1731. Willis is described on pp 235-6.

Nineteenth century publications

Aikin, John. *General Biography*, Vol 10. London: 1815. Willis is described on pp 127-9.

Bayle, ALJ and Thillaye, AJ. *Biographic Médicale par Ordre Chronologique d'Après Daniel Leclerc, Eloy, etc..* Tome 1. Paris: 1855. Willis is referred to on pp 462-3.

Biographie Universelle, Ancienne et Moderne, Tome 50. Paris: 1827. Willis is described on pp 591-4.

Calmeil, LF. *De la Folio . . .*, Tome 1. Paris: 1845. Willis's findings in brain pathology are described on pp 387-407.

Eckhard, Conrad. *Beiträge zur Anatomie und Physiologie*, Band 10. 1883. The accessory nerve of Willis is described on pp 171-203.

Fiessinger, Ch. *La Thérapeutique des Vieux Maîtres*. Paris: 1897. The therapies employed by Willis are described on pp 163-9.

Foster, J. *Alumni Oxoniensis*, 1500-1714, 4 Vols. Oxford: 1891.

Haeser, Heinrich. *Lehrbuch der Geschichte der Medicin und der epidemischen Krankheiten*, 3e Bearb, 3 Bde. Jena: 1875-1882. Willis is described in Vol 2 on pp 382-5.

Jourdan, AJL. *Dictionaire des Sciences Médicales. Biographie Médicale*, Tome 7. Paris: 1825. Willis is described on pp 505-7.

Munk, W. *The Roll of the Royal College of Physicians of London*, 2nd edn, Vol 1. London: 1878. Willis appears on pp 338-42.

Neuburger, Max. *Die historische Entwicklung der experimentellen Gehirt-und Rückenmarksphysiologie vor Flourens*. Stuttgart: 1897. Willis's theories of localisation of function in the nervous system are described.

Nouvelle Biographie Général. . ., Tome 46. Paris: 1866. Willis is described in columns 755-6.

Poggendorff, JC. *Biographisch-literarisches Handwörterbuch zur Geschichte der exacten Wissenschaften*, Bande 2. Leipzig: 1863. Willis is described in column 1332.

Richardson, Sir Benjamin War. Thomas Willis MD, FRS. In: *The Asclepiad*. Vol IX, 1892, pp 55-89. This work was reprinted with a portrait of Willis in the author's *Disciples of Aesculapius*, Vol 11. London: 1900, pp 592-616.

Soury, Jules. *Le Système Nerveux Central*, 2 tomes. Paris; 1899. Discussion of Willis's anatomical discoveries and physiological theories are in Vol 1 on pp 428-42.

Twentieth century publications

Adams, EW. Thomas Willis, MA, MD (AD. 1621-1675). *Medical Library and Historical Journal*, 1903, Vol 1, pp 265-70.

Alajouanine, Th and Bourguignon A. La première description de la myasthénie. *La Presse Médicale*, 1954, Vol 62, pp 519-20. The authors attribute the first description of myasthenia to Willis.

Allan, FN. The writings of Thomas Willis, M.D.: Diabetes three hundred years ago. *Diabetes*, 1953, Vol 2, pp 74-8.

Allen, Phyllis. Scientific studies in the English universities of the Seventeenth Century. *Journal of History and Ideas*, 1949, Vol 10, pp 219-53.

Allen, Phyllis. Medical Education in 17th Century England. *Journal of History of Medicine and Allied Science*, 1946, Vol 1, pp 115-43.

Anderson, HG. The Life of Thomas Willis, MD (The Wix Prize Essay). *St Bartholomew's Hospital Journal*, 1920, Vol 28, pp 170-3.

Anson, BJ. Thomas Willis's Anatomy of the Brain. *Quarterly Bulletin of Northwestern University Medical School* 1941, Vol 15, pp 139-51.

Anson, BJ. Thomas Willis's Treatise on Plague Remedies. *Quarterly Bulletin of Northwestern University Medical School*, 1941, Vol 15, pp 218-31.

Ashley Smith, JW. *The Birth of Modern Education. The contribution of the Dissenting Academies*, 1660-1800. London: 1954.

Aylmer, GE. *The Interregnum: The Quest for Settlement, 1646-1660*. London: 1973.

Bailey, H and Bishop, WJ. *Notable Names in Medicine and Surgery*. London: 1959. Willis is described on pp 11-12.

Barrett, CRB. *History of the Society of Apothecaries of London*. London: 1905.

Bastholm, E. The history of muscle physiology from the natural philosophers to Albrecht von Haller. *Acta Historia Scientiarum Naturalium et Medicinalium, Copenhagen*, 1950, Vol 7, pp 202-9.

Bates, D. Thomas Willis and the Epidemic Fever of 1661. *Bulletin of The History of Medicine*, 1965, Vol 39, pp 393-414.

Baumann, ED. *Francois de la Boe Sylvius*. Leiden: EJ Brill, 1949.

Bayon, HP. William Harvey, Physician and Biologist, *Annals of Science*, 1939, Vol 4, pp 329-89.

Berrios, GE. Dementia during the seventeenth and eighteenth centuries: a conceptual history. *Psychological Medicine*, 1987, Vol 17, pp 829-37.

Boas, Marie. *Robert Boyle and Seventeenth Century Chemistry*. Cambridge, Mass: University Press, 1958.

Bogaert, L van and Padermecker J. L'évolution de nos connaissances sur la myasthénie de Thomas Willis à Walker. *Acta Neurologica et Psychiatrica Belgica*, 1955, Vol 55, pp 288-308.

Brown, TM. Physiology and the mechanical philosophy in mid-seventeenth century England. *Bulletin of the History of Medicine*, 1977, Vol 51, pp 25-54.

Bulloch, W. *The History of Bacteriology*. Oxford: Oxford University Press, 1960.

Burrows, M (ed). *Register of the Visitors of the University of Oxford from A.D. 1647 to A.D. 1658 (Camden Society)*, Vol 29. London: 1881.

Bynum, WF. The anatomical method, natural theology, and the functions of the brain. *Isis*, 1973, Vol 64, pp 445-68.

Canguilhem, G. La formation du concept de réflexe par Thomas Willis. La formation du concept de mouvement reflexe aux XVIIe et XVIIIe siècles, Chap 3. *Bibliothèque de Philosophie Contemporaine*. Paris: 1955, pp 57-78.

Castiglioni, A. *A history of Medicine*, 2nd edn. Translated from the Italian and edited by EB Krumbhaar. New York: 1947. Willis is referred to on pp 541-2.

Caughey, JE. Akathisia (restless legs). *New Zealand Medical Journal*, 1987, p 121.

Caulfield, E. A Full view of all the diseases incident to children also recording an early case of infantile cerebral hemorrhage the earliest pediatric anthology. *Annals of Medical History*, 1928, Vol 10, pp 407-16.

Clark, A. *The Life and Times of Anthony Wood*, 5 Vols. Oxford: Oxford Historical Society, 1891-1900.

Clark, A and Boase, CW. *Register of the University of Oxford*, 2 Vols. Oxford: Oxford Historical Society, 1885-1889.

Clark, B. *Mental Disorder in Earlier Britain*. Cardiff: University of Wales Press, 1975.

Clark, G. *Science and Social Welfare in the Age of Newton*, 2nd edn. Oxford: 1949.

Clark, G. *A History of the Royal College of Physicians of London*, 2 Vols. Oxford: 1964-1966.

Cole, FJ. *A History of Comparative Anatomy from Aristotle to the Eighteenth Century*. London: 1944. Willis's work is described on pp 222-31.

Contributors to Science of Medicine (unsigned). Thomas Willis, *Medical Journal and Record*, 1927, Vol 126, pp 177-9.

Cooper, CH. *Annals of Cambridge*, 5 Vols. Cambridge: 1842-1908.

Costello, WJ. *The Scholastic Curriculum at Early 17th Century Cambridge*. Cambridge, Mass: 1958.

Cranefield, PF. A seventeenth century view of mental deficiency and schizophrenia: Thomas Willis on 'stupidity or foolishness'. *Bulletin of the History of Medicine*, 1961, Vol 35, pp 2912-316.

Creighton, C. *A History of Epidemics in Britain*. Reprinted London: Frank Cass, 1965. Willis's description of an epidemic of typhus appears on pp 547-52.

Curtiss, MH. *Oxford and Cambridge in Transition*, 1558-1642. Oxford: 1959.

Davis, Audrey B. Some Implications of the Circulation Theory for Disease Theory and Treatment in the Seventeenth Century. *Journal of the History of Medicine and Allied Science*, 1971, Vol 26, pp 28-39.

De Lint, JG. *Atlas of the History of Medicine. 1. Anatomy*. London: 1926, p.67.

Debus, A. Fire Analysis and the Elements in the 16th and 17th Centuries. *Annals of Science*, 1967, Vol 23, pp 127-45.

Debus, A. Paracelsian doctrine in English medicine, *Chemistry in the Service of Medicine*. Edited by FNL Poynter. Philadelphia: Lippincott, 1963.

Debus, AG. *The English Paracelsians*. London: 1965.

Debus, AG. *Science and Education in the Seventeenth Century: The Webster-Ward Debate*. London: 1970.

Debus, AG (ed). *Science, Medicine and Society in the Renaissance. Essays to Honour Walter Pagel*, 2 Vols. New York: 1972.

Dewhurst, K. An Oxford medical student's notebook. *Oxford Medical School Gazette*, 1959, Vol 2, pp 141-5.

Dewhurst, K. *John Locke: Physician and Philosopher, A Medical Biography*. London: Wellcombe Historical Medical Library, 1963.

Dewhurst, K. Willis in Oxford: some new manuscripts. *Proceedings of The Royal Society of Medicine*, 1964, Vol 58, pp 682-7.

Dewhurst, K. *Thomas Willis as a Physician*. Los Angeles: William Andrews Clark Memorial Library, University of California, 1964.

Dewhurst, K. Some letters of Thomas Willis (1621-1675), *Medical History*, 1972, Vol 16, pp 63-76.

Dewhurst, K. *Thomas Willis's Oxford Lectures*. Oxford: Sandford Publications, 1980.

Dewhurst, K. *Willis's Oxford Casebook (1650-52)*. Oxford: Sandford Publications, 1981.

Dictionary of National Biography, Vol 62. London: 1900, pp 25-6. Notice on Willis was written by Sir Norman Moore.

D'Irsay, S. Der philosophische Hintergrund der Nervenphysiologie im 17. u. 18 Jahrhundert. *Archiv. für Geschichte Medicine*, 1928, Vol 20, pp 181-97.

Dow, RS. Thomas Willis (1621-1675) as a Comparative Neurologist. *Annals of Medical History*, 1940, Vol 2, pp 181-94.

Ellis, FG. The aetiology and treatment of achalasia of the cardia. (Hunterian Lecture delivered at the Royal College of Surgeons of England). *Annals of the Royal College of Surgeons, England*, 1962, Vol 30, pp 155-82.

The Encyclopaedia Britannica, Vol 28, 11th edn. Cambridge: 1911, p687.

Faller, A. Die Präparation der weissen Substanz des Gehirns bei Stensen, Willis und Vieussens. *Gesnerus* 1982, Vol 39, pp 171-93.

Feindel, W. Restoration of memorial to Dr Thomas Willis (1621-1675) in Westminster Abbey. *British Medical Journal*, 1962, Vol 1, pp 552-3.

Fishman, AP. *Circulation of the Blood: Men and Ideas*. Edited by DW Richards. Oxford: Oxford University Press, 1964.

Foster, Sir Michael. *Lectures on the History of Physiology During the Sixteenth, Seventeenth, and Eighteenth Centuries*. Cambridge: 1901. An account of Willis's work in neurophysiology appears on pp 269-80.

Frank, RG Jr. John Aubrey, FRS, John Lydall, and science at Commonwealth Oxford. *Notes and Records of the Royal Society*, 1973, Vol 27, pp 193-217.

Frank, RG Jr. Science, medicine and the universities of early modern England: background and sources, Parts 1 and 2. *History of Science*, 1973, Vol 11, pp 194-216, 239-69.

Frank, RG Jr. The John Ward diaries: mirror of seventeenth century science and medicine. *History of Medicine*, 1974, Vol 29, pp 147-79.

Frank, R. G. Jr. *Harvey and the Oxford Physiologists*. Berkeley, Los Angeles, and London. University of California Press, 1980.

Fulton, JF. *Muscular Contraction and the Reflex Control of Movement*. London: 1926. Willis's theories of muscle contraction appear on pp 17-21.

Garraud, RM. Thomas Willis et les anatomistes d'Oxford. *La Presse medicale*, 1954, Vol 62, pp 481-2.

Garrison, FH. *An Introduction to the History of Medicine with Medical Chronology, Suggestions for Study and Bibliographic Data*, 4th edn. Philadelphia: 1929. Willis is described on pp 262-4.

Gotch, F. *Two Oxford Physiologists: Richard Lower 1631-1691, John Mayow 1643-1679*. Oxford: 1908. Willis is referred to on pp 5-8 and 17-18.

Gunther, RT. *Early science in Oxford. The Biological Sciences*, Vol 3. Oxford: 1925. Willis is described on pp 59-63 and 96-103.

Gurdjian, ES and Gurdjian ES. History of Occlusive Cerebrovascular Disease, Part 1. *Archives of Neurology*, 1979, Vol 36, pp 340-3.

Gibson, WC (Ed). *British Contributions to Medical Science: The Woodward-Wellcome Symposium at the University of British Columbia, 1970*. London: Wellcome Institute of the History of Medicine, 1971.

Guthrie, D. *A History of Medicine*. London: 1958. Willis is described on p 200.

Hargreaves-Maudsley, WN. *Oxford in the Age of John Locke*. Norman, Oklahoma: University of Oklahoma Press, 1973.

Hartley, H. *The Royal Society, its Origins and Founders*. London: The Royal Society, 1960.

Hierons, R. Willis's contributions to clinical medicine and neurology. *Journal of Neurology and Science*, 1967, Vol 4, pp 1-13.

Hierons, R and Meyer A. Some priority questions arising from Thomas Willis' work on the brain. *Proceedings of the Royal Society of Medicine*, 1961, Vol 55, pp 287-2.

Heroes of medicine (unsigned) Thomas Willis. *The Practitioner*, 1900, Vol 65, pp 166-70.

Hirsch, A (Ed). *Biographisches Lexikon der hervorragenden Ärzte*, 2 Aufl, Band 5. Berlin and Wien: 1935. Willis is described on p 947.

Hoff, EB and Hoff, PM. The life and times of Richard Lower, physiologist and physician (1631-1691). *Bulletin of the Inst of the History of Medicine*, 1936, Vol 4, pp 517-35.

Hoff, HE and Kellaway, P. The early history of the reflex. *Journal of the History of Medicine and Allied Science*, 1952, Vol 7, pp 211-249. Willis is described on pp 221-3.

Horsley, Sir Victor. *The Cerebellum: Its Relation to Spatial Orientation and to Locomotion (The Boyle Lecture for 1905)*. London: 1905. Willis's work is described on pp 8-13 and 29-31.

Hughes, JT. Spinal cord arteries described by Willis, Chap 20. In: *Historical Aspects of the Neurosciences*, edited by FC Rose and WF Bynum. New York: Raven Press, 1982.

Hughes, JT. Thomas Willis: the first Oxford neuropathologist. In: *Neuroscience Across the Centuries*, edited by FC Rose. London: Smith-Gordon; Niigata: Nishimura, 1989.

Hughes, JT. Miraculous deliverance of Anne Green: an Oxford case of resuscitation in the seventeenth century. *British Medical Journal*, 1982, Vol 285, pp 1792-3.

Innes Smith, RW. *English Speaking Students of Medicine at the University of Leyden*. Edinburgh: 1932.

Isler, H. *Thomas Willis, 1621-1675: Doctor and Scientist*. New York and London: Hafner Publishing Company, 1968.

Jobe, TH. Medical theories of melancholia in the seventeenth and early eighteenth centuries. *Clio Medico*, 1976, Vol 11, pp 217-31.

Jones, GW. Robert Boyle as a medical man. *Bulletin of the History of Medicine*, 1964, Vol 38, pp 139-52.

Keynes, Sir Geoffrey. The history of myasthenia gravis. *Medical History*, 1961, Vol 5, pp 313-26.

Lennox, WG. Thomas Willis on narcolepsy. *Archives of Neurology and Psychiatry*, 1939, Vol 41, pp 348-51.

Levy-Valensi, J. La neuro-psychiatrie au XVIIe siècle. 1., *Paris Medicine*, Vol 1, pp 374-83. Willis's work is described on pp 379-383.

Lippman, EO von. *Abhandlungen und Vorträge zur Geschichte der Naturwissenschaften*. Leipzig: 1906. Willis's observations on diabetes mellitus appear on pp 329-30.

Long, E. *A History of Pathology*. London: 1928. Willis is described on pp 90-2.

Major, RH. *Classic Descriptions of Disease with Biographical Sketches of the Authors*. London: 1932. Willis's contributions are recognised widely throughout this work, and the page numbers are given. Epidemics, pp 121-4; putrid fever, pp 132-6; biography, pp 191; polyuria, pp 192-4; pleurisy, pp 534-6; asthma, pp 541-5; and vomiting, pp 591-3.

McKie, D. The origins and foundation of the Royal Society of London. *Notes and Records of the Royal Society*, 1960, Vol 15, pp 1-37.

Meier, RY. 'Sympathy' in the neurophysiology of Thomas Willis. *Clio Medica*. 1982, Vol 17, pp 95-111.

Merton, RK. *Science, Technology, and Society in Seventeenth Century England*. New York: 1970.

Meyer, A. Karl Friedrich Burdach on Thomas Willis. *Journal of Neurological Science*, 1966, Vol 3, pp 109-16.

Meyer, A. *Historical Aspects of Cerebral Anatomy*. London, New York, Toronto; Oxford University Press, 1971.

Meyer, A. The concept of a sensorimotor cortex. Its early history, with especial emphasis on two early experimental contributions by W Bechterew. *Brain*, 1978, Vol 101, pp 673-85.

Meyer, A. Historical Survey. The concept of a sensorimotor cortex: its later history during the twentieth century. *Neuropathology and Applied Neurobiology*, 1982, Vol 8, pp 81-93.

Meyer, A and Hierons, R. Observations on the history of the 'Circle of Willis'. *Medical History*, 1962, Vol 6, pp 119-30.

Meyer, A and Hierons, R. On Thomas Willis's concepts of Neurophysiology, Parts 1 and 2. *Medical History*, 1965, Vol 9, pp 1-15 and 142-55.

Miller, WS. Thomas Willis and his *De Phthisi Pulmonari, American Review of Tuberculosis*, 1922, Vol 5, pp 934-59.

Miller, WS. Thomas Willis (1621-1675). *Bulletin of the Society of Medical History, Chicago*, 1923-1925, Vol 3, pp 215-32.

Miller, WS. *The Lung*. London: 1937. Willis's observations on pulmonary disease are described on pp 86-7 and 152-4.

Moore, Sir Norman, *The Circle of Willis*. London: 1911.

Nordenskiold, E. *The History of Biology: a Survey*. London: 1929. Willis's work is described on pp 148-50.

Ogg, D. *England in the Reign of Charles II*, 2nd edn, Vol 2. Oxford: 1956. Willis's part in this historical period is described on pp 717-18.

Papaspyros, NS. *The History of Diabetes Mellitus*. London: 1952. Willis's part in the discovery of diabetes is dealt with on pp 10-11.

Partington, JR. *A History of Chemistry*, Vol 2. London: 1961. Willis's use of iatrochemistry is described on pp 304-11.

Power, Sir D'Arcy. John Ward and his diary – Part 1 (Presidential address). *Transactions of the Medical Society of London*, 1917, Vol 40, pp 1-26.

Purver, M. *The Royal Society: Concept and Creation*. London: 1967.

Rasmussen, AT. *Some Trends in Neuroanatomy*. Iowa: Dubuque, 1947. Willis's work is described on pp 10-12.

Rattansi, PM. The Helmontian-Galenist controversy in Restoration England. *Ambix*, 1964, Vol 12, pp 1-23.

Rattansi, PM. Paracelsus and the Puritan Revolution. *Ambix*, 1963, Vol 11, pp 24-32.

Robb-Smith, AHT. Harvey at Oxford. *Oxford Medical Students Gazette*, 1957, Vol 9, pp 70-6.

Rolleston, Sir Humphry. Thomas Willis. *Medical Life*, 1934, Vol 41, pp 177-91.

Rossi, P. *Francis Bacon. From Magic to Science*. London: 1968.

Schoenberg DG and Schoenberg BS. The death of the birth of neurology: The neurologic contributions of Thomas Willis. *Surgery and Neurology*, 1975, Vol 4, pp 401-6.

Schoenberg, DG and Schoenberg, BS. Eponym: rounds with Dr Thomas Willis. *Southern Medical Journal*, 1976, Vol 69, pp 941-2.

Sheehan, D. Discovery of the autonomic nervous system. *Archives of Neurology and Psychiatry*, 1936, Vol 35, pp 1081-115.

Sinclair, HM and Robb-Smith, AHT. *A Short History of Anatomical Teaching in Oxford*. Oxford: 1950.

Stirling, W. *Some Apostles of Physiology*. London: 1902.

Stevenson, WH. *The Early History of St John's College, Oxford*, New Series, Vol 1. Oxford: Oxford Historical Society, Clarendon Press, 1939.

Stolkind, E. The history of bronchial asthma and allergy. *Proceedings of the Royal Society of Medicine*, 1933, Vol 26, pp 1120-6. Willis's recognition of the state of asthma is described on p 1123.

Swayne, D. *The Story of North Hinksey*. North Hinksey, Oxford: Published by the author, 1973.

Syfret, RH. The origins of the Royal Society. *Notes and Records of the Royal Society*, 1947, Vol 5, pp 75-137.

Symonds, C. The Circle of Willis (Harveian Oration). *British Medical Journal*, 1955, Vol 12, pp 119-24.

Symonds, C. Thomas Willis, FRS (1621-1675). *Notes and Records of the Royal Society of London*, 1960, Vol 15, pp 91-7.

Symonds, C. Thomas Willis FRS (1621-1675). In: *The Royal Society: Its Origins and Founders*, edited by Sir Harold Hartley. London: 1960.

Symonds, C and Feindel W. Birthplace of Thomas Willis. *British Medical Journal*, 1969, Vol 3, pp 648-9.

Temkin, O. *The Falling Sickness: As History of Epilepsy From the Greeks to the Beginnings of Modern Neurology*. Monograph IV, First Series. Baltimore: Institute of the History of Medicine, The Johns Hopkins University, 1945. Willis's descriptions of epilepsy appear on pp 196-9 and 210-11.

Thorndike, L. *A History of Magic and Experimental Science*, Vols VII and VIII. New York: 1958. Willis's work is described in Vol 7 on pp 519-20 and in Vol 8 on pp 207-8, 356-7, 520-1, and 524-7.

Thornton, JL. *Medical Books, Libraries and Collectors: a Study of Bibliography and the Book Trade in Relation to Medical Sciences*. London: 1949. Willis's books are referred to on pp 65-6.

Tizard, B. Theories of brain localization from Flourens to Lashley. *Medical History*, 1959, Vol 3, pp 132-45.

Viets, Sir Henry. A patronal festival for Thomas Willis (1621-1675) with remarks by Sir William Osler. *Annals of Medical History*, 1917, Vol 1, pp 118-24.

Vinchon, J and Vie, J. Un maitre de la neuropsychiatrie au XVIIe siècle: Thomas Willis, (1621-1675). *Annals of Medicine and Psychology*, 1928, Vol 86, pp 109-44.

Webster, C. English medical reformers of the puritan revolution: a background to the 'Society of Chymical Physitians'. *Ambix*, 1967, Vol 14, pp 16-41.

Webster, C. The College of Physicians: 'Solomon's House' in Commonwealth England. *Bulletin of the History of Medicine*, 1967, Vol 41, pp 393-412.

Webster, C. The origins of the Royal Society. *History of Science*, 1967, Vol 6, pp 106-28.

Webster, C. New light on the Invisible College: The social relations of English science in the mid-seventeenth century. *Transactions of the Royal Historical Society*, 1974, Vol 24, pp 19-42.

Webster, C. *The Great Instauration: Science, Medicine and Reform 1626-1660*. London: Duckworth, 1975.

Wells, WA. Dr Thomas Willis (1621-1675): a great seventeenth century English anatomist and clinician who anticipated many modern discoveries. *The Laryngoscope*, 1949, Vol 59, pp 287-305.

Welton, TS. Circle of Willis (Biographical Brevities). *American Journal of Surgery*, 1929, Vol 7, p 136.

Wightman, WPD. Wars of ideas in neurological science – from Willis to Bichat and from Locke to Condillac. In: *The History and Philosophy of Knowledge of the Brain and its Functions*. Anglo-American Symposium held in London, 15-17 July 1957. Oxford: Wellcombe Historical Library, 1958.

Williamson, RT. *English Physicians of the Past*. Newcastle-upon-Tyne: 1923.

Wing, D. *Short-title Catalogue of Books Printed in England 1641-1700*, 5 Vols. New York: 1945-1951.

Wing, HJR. A bibliography of Dr Thomas Willis (1621-1675). Thesis submitted to the University of London, 1962.

Woolham, DHM. The historical significance of the cerebro-spinal fluid. *Medical History*, 1957, Vol 1, pp 91-114.

Young, J. Willis. *New England Medical Journal*, 1923, Vol 22, pp 141-9.

INDEX